T0279914

The Privacy Pirates:
How Your Privacy is Being Stolen and What You Can Do About It

Leslie N. Gruis

The Privacy Pirates:
How Your Privacy is Being Stolen and What You Can Do About It

Leslie N. Gruis

Academica Press
Washington~London

Library of Congress Cataloging-in-Publication Data

Names: Gruis, Leslie N., author.
Title: The privacy pirates : how your privacy is being stolen and what
you can do about it | Leslie N. Gruis
Description: Washington : Academica Press, 2023
Identifiers: LCCN 2023904543 | ISBN 9781680538250 (hardcover) |
9781680538267 (paperback) | 9781680538274 (ebook)

*This book is dedicated to P, the world's most fabulous feline,
my faithful companion and muse*

Contents

Preface

I wrote this book for every American. It explains where the spirit of privacy comes from, why it is essential to democracy, and what we can do to preserve both.

I spent thirty years as an intelligence officer at the National Security Agency. Initially recruited as a mathematician, I was called on to explain the capabilities of new technologies to our attorneys. I worked closely with them to ensure that our technologies both met our national security needs and preserved our civil rights. Over the course of my career, my legal and policy experience grew. After an assignment at the National Intelligence Council, and as I prepared to retire, I realized how privileged I'd been to see the privacy debate evolve from the inside. I wanted to share what I'd seen with others.

As I sat down to write this book, I found privacy hard to define because it was a value I had been raised with. It was one of those things I felt in my gut but couldn't explain. Privacy, I realized, was the unseen force at the core of American rights.

I went looking for the word "privacy" in our founding documents. It wasn't in the Declaration of Independence or the US Constitution. Over time, I realized it was there as an *implied* value. I felt its spirit most strongly in the US Bill of Rights.

What I learned from all this is that our democracy's success requires it to adapt to changing times while still preserving individual rights. In the appendix, I've looked at how the definitions of many legal terms evolved to retain their original intent, like the freedom from search and seizure enshrined in the Fourth Amendment.

Congress has passed many laws to safeguard our privacy from high-tech intrusion. However, the law has yet to catch up with the "Privacy

Pirates," companies that monetize your private information by using internet technologies. These marauders remain free to exploit your and my privacy and erode our democracy. After over thirty years in the business, I've concluded that it's the Privacy Pirates, not our government, who pose the greatest risk to our privacy and way of life.

Welcome to the privacy journey. Let's get started.

Chapter 1

Privacy is Dead

"Criminy Dutch, girl!"

Alice's grandmother put the cell phone down on the kitchen counter as though it had suddenly become infectious.

"This picture. What were you thinkin'?" she continued.

"It's nothing, Grandma," replied Alice. "It's just me and my friends at the beach."

"Girl." Grandma Ruby shook her head. "What are you wearin'? You're naked."

"The boys can't see it, Grandma. I told you. It's just a private post. For my friends."

"You sure of that? You sure nobody can get to it? On the computer? Because you also said," Grandma Ruby peered at the screen, adjusting her glasses, "where you were, all your names, where you were goin' next, someone's birthday . . ."

Alice took back her iPhone and slipped it into her jeans. Her lower lip was poking out, and she looked about ten years younger than her actual age of fourteen. Alice loved her grandmother very much, but sometimes old people could be a real pain. They were so stupid about some things.

"Sweetie, don't be angry with your grandmother." Alice's mom, Mary, walked into the kitchen carrying two over-full plastic shopping bags. "And help me out, would you? There's more in the hall."

"I'm not being angry! You just don't understand. Everybody posts everything. Just because you don't—"

"You think nobody's spyin' on you?" Grandma Ruby looked at Alice over the top of her bifocals in a way that Alice found particularly infuriating. "Really? I lived through the Cold War, child. Roosians spyin' on everyone, everywhere. Do you really think spyin's stopped? With all them new gadgets they've got these days? That Interweb, and all that other—"

"It's the internet, Grandma." Alice rolled her eyes. "And privacy is dead. Nobody cares anymore. That was your and mom's generation, not mine."

"Hey, your grandma and I are from different generations!" responded Mary, looking at her daughter with just a hint of a smile.

"I don't care," Alice snapped back. "I should've never shown you that selfie. You guys are, like, dinosaurs. Privacy is dead. Deader than the dodo bird. It's the age of social media now, and it belongs to us, and you guys are just too out of touch to ever get it."

And with that brief speech completed, Alice turned on her heel, phone sticking out of her back pocket, and headed to the hallway where more bags of groceries were waiting.

Grandma Ruby turned to her middle-aged daughter. "Girl certainly knows how to make an exit, I'll give her that."

"Mom . . . ," Mary gestured helplessly. "I wish you two wouldn't argue so . . ."

But Grandma Ruby was shaking her head. "Arguin's about opinion," she proclaimed. "This ain't opinion. People been spyin' on each other since the first caveman followed the second caveman to figure out where the good huntin' was. Just naivety, that's all it is." Ruby put her glasses back in the case—she was far too vain to wear them around her neck—and snapped the lid shut with finality.

"Maybe she really doesn't care about privacy, Mom. Maybe it's just a different gener—"

"Oh, she cares. Jiminy crickets. She cares a lot, a whole lot." Grandma Ruby shuffled toward the kitchen door as fast as her bad hip would allow. Then she turned her head back to her daughter and smiled.

"Just ain't old enough to know what she really cares about, that's all."

Mary shrugged. Alone in the kitchen, she began unpacking the groceries.

*   *   *   *   *

The Privacy Pirates are out there, whether we can see them or not. The reason couldn't be simpler. Billions of dollars are at stake.

Giant companies like Amazon, Facebook, and Instagram are not inherently evil, but they're not on your side either. These companies exist for the same reason all companies exist. They are there to make money. That's the number one thing Alice in our story doesn't understand, yet.

Like many Americans, Alice thinks she lives in a modern moment. Services like Facebook, Twitter, Pinterest, and Instagram are there to meet her needs and simplify her life, and there's no real price to pay. In reality, Alice is in the grip of a modern privacy exploitation machine. The value of the assets she owns—currently being pirated—is significant, and the net invasion of privacy is colossal.

The media are not innocent either, neither mainstream nor social. They aren't there primarily to manipulate or lie to us. Sometimes, they tell the absolute truth. But the primary purpose of a media company is the same as that of any other company; it's there to sell a product and make a profit.

The liberties companies take with your private information— some harmless, others sinister—are all driven by the profit motive.

When I was in the intelligence community, they always used to tell us to follow the money. It turns out that both money and dead bodies can be hard to hide. We won't meet any dead bodies here, but we'll need to remember that the profit motive is always paramount.

You know that the Privacy Pirates—the Googles, Amazons, and Facebooks of the world—are collecting your private information right now, every time you touch the internet. You might be looking up the Magna Carta (Google), searching for a new space heater (Amazon), or finding out whether your cousin Sally finally had that baby (Facebook).

The Privacy Pirates take all the information you share with them and combine it with the vital information of millions of others. They put this information into their fancy artificial intelligence (AI) technologies. These technologies allow them to suck all the value out of your and everyone else's information. They use it to make money.

One of the AI outputs is predictions about your behavior. The Privacy Pirates use this information to target your interests with the advertising they send you. They craft each ad to convince you that this purchase will bring you closer to happiness. True, sometimes the ads lead you to buy useful things, like the perfect dog bed for your pooch. But sometimes, these ads get you to purchase stuff you don't need, like that amazing Kanji knife. You thought it would simplify chopping, but now it just collects dust in the bottom of your kitchen drawer.

AI outputs also allow the Privacy Pirates to treat your private information like a commodity, like gold or soybeans. They want to sell and trade it with others to—you guessed it—make money. These Privacy Pirates see your privacy as an obstacle to getting richer and richer. They're happy to ignore, sidestep, or "overlook" any privacy rights you might have so they can make a buck.

I'm here to tell you that this must stop.

In this book, we will learn why privacy is vital to democracy. If you value your democratic freedoms, it's your responsibility as a citizen to push back.

Now you might think I'm exaggerating. How could the fate of democracy possibly hinge on our use of the internet? Well, we read every day how governments and trolls use the internet to sway the outcomes of elections. Do you think that undermines democracy? We routinely see how disinformation campaigns spread lies and cause dissent and panic. Do you still doubt the power of the internet to distort the truth and undermine your freedoms?

Privacy has been with us since the beginning of our US history and has evolved slowly in thought, practice, and law. It has been challenged significantly by communications technologies. The internet is the latest technology to challenge privacy and our democracy.

So, turn the page, and I'll start trying to persuade you. I intend to give you a convincing argument that may change your thinking or may help you change the thinking of others.

Privacy is a muscle. Use it or lose it. Without regular use, it will atrophy and waste away. Reading this book will give you the information you need to stand up for privacy and support the democracy you love.

Chapter 2

What's Privacy?

"She looks old, doesn't she?" said Mary, leaning against her husband Scott in the front doorway.

"Well, she's not," Scott replied abruptly. "She's just a kid. Our kid."

Alice turned to wave from the curb and got into an old Honda Civic. The ancient car coughed once or twice and then vanished into the advancing evening.

"And that kid doesn't look old enough to shave, much less drive," Scott continued.

"Oh, relax. He's a good kid. You've known him since he was a baby. They're meeting friends."

Mary and Scott closed the front door and headed to the sofa for a night of Netflix. Both were quiet, thinking about their daughter.

"She is alright, isn't she?" ventured Mary.

Scott nodded. "Yeah, I think so." Mary reached for the remote control and turned on the plasma TV mounted on the wall. "She's got a good head on her shoulders, I think," continued Scott. And then they both laughed.

"We're getting old," said Mary.

"That we are. I mean, back in my day, I worried about my parents snooping in my room. For drugs. Or contraceptives. Or porn."

Scott and Mary both laughed again, this time a little more nervously.

"But they never did snoop through your room, did they?" asked Mary.

"Good lord, no. We had different views about privacy in those days. If they had and I'd found out, it would have destroyed our relationship. And then I might've really gone off the rails and gotten into some serious trouble."

"But it's a different age now, isn't it?" mused Mary. "You heard Alice. She doesn't give a hoot about privacy. Dead and buried, she said. So, wouldn't you at least like to know if your daughter is on the pill? They don't need our permission anymore to get it, remember."

"Well, isn't that a bit sexist?" replied Scott. "But yeah, I remember. Both my sister and I were already doing foolish things at Alice's age. We were lucky to get away with them. Our parents probably *should've* gone through our rooms."

Mary stood up. "It won't take a minute," she said, tilting her head toward the end of the hall where their daughter's room was. "And my mind's made up."

Mary and Scott spent the next two hours watching Jane Fonda, Jack Lemmon, and Michael Douglas in *The China Syndrome*. Both had forgotten what a good movie it was. Alice came home around ten, offered the usual monosyllabic response about how her evening had been, and headed to her room, pleading exhaustion. Scott poured another glass of red for Mary, then one for himself.

"You assholes!" came a sudden voice. Scott and Mary both jumped—Alice had come up behind them without warning.

"Hey!" snapped Scott. "Don't use language like—"

"You assholes!" yelled Alice even louder. Tears were streaming down her face, her as-yet unremoved mascara streaking. With her hair askew and her face red with rage, Alice looked like a demented avenging goddess.

"You went through my room!" shouted Alice. "Everything's been moved! You think I wouldn't notice?"

"Honey . . . ," began Mary, in the voice she'd used to soothe tantrums when Alice was two. "We just want to keep you safe, OK? And we thought you'd be OK with that. I mean, young people today . . . you said it yourself . . . they don't really care about privacy, right? So, your dad and I—"

"Not like that! Not like that! Of course I care if you go looking through my private things! How could you? How could you be so stupid?"

"Honey," tried Scott, in his own version of the Alice-tantrum-soothing voice.

"Honey, nothing!" Alice yelled back. "You snooped on me. You don't trust me. How would you like it? You don't think my privacy is worth anyth—"

"Pumpkin, we were just trying to keep you—"

"I don't want to hear it!" Exit Alice, still in tears, followed by the sound of a slamming door, and then the scraping of something being put up against her door so no one could open it.

A long moment passed.

"Give her about fifteen minutes," said Mary. "Then I'll go talk to her."

Scott nodded. Then he gave his wife a consoling hug and smiled ruefully.

"People are strange, aren't they?" he said as he picked up his wineglass.

*   *   *   *   *

Different generations see privacy differently. For someone like Alice, who grew up with computers and the internet, privacy appears to be a non-issue in cyberspace. It's just the way things are. To her, it's normal to post lots of information about her activities and movements. That's how she stays connected with her friends. It's also how she keeps up with the latest trends and gossip.

On the other hand, Alice does value physical privacy. She feels like her parents violated her privacy by searching her room. Alice thinks they are creeps for having done it and can see no rational reason for their actions. She no longer trusts them like she used to because they took advantage—at least, as she sees it.

Alice's parents didn't grow up with the internet. They think it's strange that Alice and her peers share so much information about themselves in cyberspace. They would never do that.

They're especially concerned about Alice's safety. She's a young, impressionable girl. She tries to act older than she is, but she's still a kid that needs parenting. They worry that Alice's participation in social media could make her vulnerable to predators. They've read stories.

Alice's parents value their privacy in both physical and virtual space. But Alice's privacy, in their minds, is entirely different. She's a minor child living under their roof for whom they are still responsible. They only intended to set their minds at ease by quickly searching Alice's room.

So, Alice and her parents have two very different views on what privacy is or should be. Their views illustrate how broadly American privacy beliefs and practices vary.

To US lawyers, privacy is a complicated subject. They describe it with lots of confusing words and settle on six distinct flavors of privacy:

- **Physical**: The right to be free from physical intrusion. Embodied in our Third and Fourth Amendments, physical privacy touches upon the sanctity of the home as the center of private life.
- **Decisional**: The right to make personal life choices freely without government intervention. Decisional privacy often involves personal decisions associated with birth control, abortion, gender reassignment, or assisted suicide.
- **Proprietary**: The right to use one's body as one chooses. Originating in the commercial use of a portrait without permission, proprietary privacy today extends to all unique attributes of the individual, including DNA.

- **Associational**: The right to associate privately with whom one chooses. A famous Supreme Court case upheld the right of a private group not to disclose its membership roster to the government.
- **Intellectual**: The right to think, express, and share one's thoughts without fear of government intervention.
- **Informational**: The right to share or not share your private information and have it protected from misuse or release to others without your permission.

Luckily, we don't have to understand the foregoing in great detail. In this book, we're only going to talk about informational privacy, which is the privacy of your information in physical and virtual space.

Everyone has his or her own definition of privacy. For me, privacy is the right to enjoy my physical and spiritual spaces. Such enjoyment is possible only in a democratic society where everyone respects and supports privacy. Such respect guarantees that my home is my sanctuary. It allows me to be alone with my written and unwritten thoughts. It recognizes my right to share thoughts or keep them to myself. And it should extend to my personal information in cyberspace.

So how do we understand where privacy comes from? Just as a house must be built on a sound foundation to endure, American privacy stands on a solid core of constitutional history, colonial conflict, and founding documents.

But wait a minute, you say. The word "privacy" doesn't even appear in the Declaration of Independence, the Constitution, or the Bill of Rights! What gives?

Privacy lives between the lines in our founding documents. Every time you see a word like "free," "right," or "liberty," privacy is implicitly understood. For example, you are FREE to preserve your personal privacy. You have a RIGHT to have your home respected as your castle. Your LIBERTY protects you from unwarranted search and seizure. All such terms are a secret code for the unspoken but implied concept of privacy.

Therefore, it's worth looking at our founding documents and the motivations for the words used in them to understand privacy.

In the next chapter, we'll start by considering the constitutionalism the colonists brought with them from England. Heralding back to the Magna Carta of 1215, this constitutional tradition guaranteed individual rights that the king could not ignore. Many of these are rights we still enjoy today, like due process and expressing our grievances to the government for redress.

Unfortunately, the king's respect for his subjects' rights did not extend to the colonists in the New World. The king (and his agents) denied freedom of the press, executed unauthorized search warrants, levied taxes without representation, and didn't respond to petitions for redress. The resulting Declaration of Independence presented a detailed list of the king's violations of colonists' rights.

The Federalist Papers today help us understand the publicly debated issues as our forefathers got ready to write the US Constitution. Key insights included

- using the lessons of ancient Greece to choose between a republic and a democracy for the new government;
- creating a constitution that represented a social contract between the people and the government;
- confronting the need for a standing army to address the vast nation's national security concerns;
- admitting that men were not angels and that a government administered by men had to control both the population and itself;
- ensuring that the government had an adequate source of revenue to operate;
- accepting the fact that a strong national government was essential;
- coming to terms with the issue of a bill of rights.

While unmentioned by the Federalists, privacy was an implicit element of the conversation. After all, the expectation of privacy had existed in the American psyche since colonial times. The Federalists understood that the new constitution would have to include privacy among the many "national rights, privileges, and protection[s]" (Jay, Federalist 2) to which each citizen was entitled.

This unspoken requirement appeared in the Bill of Rights. Even though the word "privacy" is missing, its spirit lives in many of the Bill of Rights amendments, including the First, Third, Fourth, Fifth, and Ninth.

The next chapter looks at the founding events of privacy in more detail, and in chronological order. Here you'll see the shadowy shape of modern privacy take form as people realized what was necessary to build a robust American republic.

First, let's catch up with Alice. Then, let's get into our imaginary time machine and travel back to the year 1215.

Chapter 3

Our Privacy Culture

"You were out of line, Mom. So was Dad." Alice poured herself a glass of orange juice and sat down at the breakfast table. "After all I do to earn your trust. It wasn't fair."

"I'm sorry, sweetie," offered Mary. "We were just trying to do the right th—"

"Yeah, yeah," replied Alice with just a trace of a smile. "And the guy who blew up the Hindenburg was probably trying to do the right thing too." She tipped some cornflakes into a bowl.

"But you violated my privacy," Alice went on. "You should've known better. I mean, you're a nurse. And dad's a lawyer, after all."

"Thanks very much," commented Mary.

"No, Mom, I didn't mean it like that," added Alice hastily. "It's just that Dad should know all about my rights, right? I mean, I know he's into international trade and all that stuff, but he should know about privacy too, right? I mean, like a brain doctor knows where the big toe is?"

"Oh, hello, you mean I actually know something?" came a booming interjection from the doorway. Scott walked into the kitchen, fiddling with his iPhone and looking distracted. "It's good to know I still know something at my age. It's a relief. I thought I was too stupid to still know anything."

"Dad . . . ," Alice protested.

"So you think we violated your rights," Scott said slowly.

"Yes!" Alice scowled at her father, suddenly looking much younger than fourteen again.

"Which ones?" replied Scott instantly.

"What do you mean which ones? All of them!" said Alice.

"Not good enough. Which rights specifically?" Scott rested his chin on one hand and looked at his daughter.

"My constitutional rights!"

"Nope."

"It's right there! In the Constitution!"

"Nope."

"The Bill of Rights, then!"

"Uh-uh." Scott grinned as he saw his daughter's bright mind beginning to really engage.

"Well, somewhere then! It's got to be somewhere."

"You still want those shoes?" replied Scott quietly.

"Huh? What?" Alice was completely thrown by this change of subject.

"The hundred-dollar Nikes. You still want them?" Scott leaned back in his chair and took a mouthful of cornflakes.

"Of course! They're super cute! But you and Mom said no . . ."

"Because we don't want a spoiled rich kid. But I will pay for work, kiddo. I'll always pay for honest work."

"I don't get it," Alice shrugged.

"You hit the books, hit the library, hit the internet," replied her father, leaning forward. "You find me exactly where the right to privacy is enshrined in the legislation. Then you write me an opinion just like a real lawyer would. And if you do a good job, I'll gladly pay you a hundred dollars."

A beat of silence went past. "I wouldn't know where to start," said Alice eventually.

"Your problem. You're a smart girl. You figure it out." And with those words, Scott walked into the living room to take a call, still carrying a half-eaten bowl of cornflakes.

Moments later, Alice left too, head bowed, scrolling intently through her iPhone.

"He's a smart one, that man o' your," said Grandma Ruby from the other side of the kitchen. She'd been sitting there quietly, listening to the conversation between them. "That girl's got a brain, and he's gonna make her use it."

"Yeah," Mary grinned, "he has his moments."

Then Mary and her mother finished their breakfasts and got on with their day.

*   *   *   *   *

Alice's father is getting off cheaply. We all have a sense that privacy must be hidden in our founding documents somewhere.

The word "privacy" means an expectation of being left alone, free from intrusion. Alice had an expectation of privacy within her bedroom; from her point of view, her parents violated that. She expected her room to be free from "search and seizure," as the Fourth Amendment says. Now Alice is about to learn that privacy is an unspoken value embedded in a tradition of individual rights that began in England long ago.

English Origins of our Constitution

Bad King John was forced to sign the Magna Carta in 1215 because his noblemen were sick and tired of the king not respecting their rights. The Magna Carta recognized the private rights of citizens related to land, taxes, inheritance, and treatment under the law. Many of the provisions of the Magna Carta—England's first constitution—would find their way into our US Constitution centuries later.

The 1600s brought constitutional crisis for England. Throughout much of the century, the kings had only outdated tax laws—laws their subjects considered abusive—to raise revenue. Parliament further controlled the monarchs by refusing to allocate any funding for the kingdom. England fell into civil war by the middle of the century and beheaded its king. Parliament restored a new king to the throne in 1660 but limited his powers and cinched the kingdom's purse strings.

Things went from bad to worse until 1688, when William and Mary ascended the throne after swearing allegiance to the new Bill of Rights (1689) passed by parliament. This bill listed all the previous king's offenses and made the new king and queen promise not to commit any of them. This new constitution prohibited the new king and queen from violating the rules of free elections and the parliamentary rights to free speech and procedure. They also had to agree not to

- act without parliamentary approval to raise taxes;
- keep a standing army during peacetime;
- quarter (give food and shelter to) soldiers in people's homes.

In the Bill of Rights, parliament codified a fundamental change to the conditions under which a king and queen were allowed to rule, affirming renewed public interest in individual rights and privacy itself. The people had spoken.

The Colonial Path to Revolution

England did not follow this Bill of Rights for its colonists in the New World. Elected representatives to parliament expressed opinions of English subjects living in England but not those of colonists. These expats rebelled in the 1760s after parliament passed new laws taxing the colonies. As a result, a new—today popular—American slogan was born: "No taxation without representation."

The British parliament also passed several other acts in the 1770s without consulting the colonists. In response to the 1773 Boston Tea Party, parliament passed an act to close the port of Boston. It also changed the original 1691 charter of the Massachusetts colony, forbidding town meetings and reducing the colony's power to govern itself. Parliament also renewed Britain's authority to require colonists to house British soldiers in people's homes. Again, the colonists objected because parliament hadn't considered the colonists' opinions on these matters. The New World colonial pot was about to boil over.

The Declaration of Independence

Angered by the king's neglect of their individual rights and privacy, colonial leaders formed the First Continental Congress in Philadelphia in 1774. They wrote and sent a petition to the king to consider their complaints and set things right. Before they received a reply, war broke out at Lexington and Concord in Massachusetts.

In 1776, the Second Continental Congress authored and approved the Declaration of Independence and sent it off to King George III. The document included a laundry list of royal offenses reminiscent of those in the English Bill of Rights. It also pointed out that the king had responded only with "repeated injury" to colonists' petitions for redress.

The Declaration of Independence focuses on the inalienable rights—implicitly including privacy—to which every individual is entitled. Individuals create governments to protect their rights and empower governments by giving up some of these rights. Should any government overstep its authority, the people have the right to alter or abolish it and create a new one to secure their safety and happiness. If the exact words aren't ringing in your ears yet, you can find them posted on the National Archives website at *https://www.archives.gov/founding-docs/declaration-transcript.*

The Federalist Papers

Today, we study the Federalist Papers because our first constitution, the Articles of Confederation, had been a flop. Drafted by the Second Continental Congress in 1777, the articles granted the government too little power to act effectively. Specifically, Congress had been too weak to collect enough funds to pay off the country's Revolutionary War debt.

The country needed a new constitution. To help the public understand the issues, three men—James Madison, Alexander Hamilton, and John Jay—wrote a series of newspaper articles. These are now known as the Federalist Papers. They contained radical thoughts about how to revise the Articles of Confederation. Embedded in these discussions were issues related to individual rights and privacy.

The real reason we read the Federalist Papers today is to get inside the heads of our forefathers. What were they thinking, and what were they trying to help the public understand? How did they arrive at the words for the new constitution? The main ideas are summarized below.

1. We can use lessons from history to think about our new form of government.

Madison (Federalist 14) noted that many of the city-states of ancient Greece had been thriving democracies. He claimed that the secret of each democracy's success had been its geographical compactness. This compactness made it easier for citizens to assemble at a central point and participate in a government of the people.

But the United States was anything but compact. In fact, it was expanding across an entire continent. What form of government might work in America?

Madison (Federalist 10) argued that a republic, instead of a democracy, would better govern a large nation. He said that "the natural limit of a republic is that distance from the centre [sic] which will barely allow the representatives to meet as often as may be necessary for the administration of public affairs." The representative government had to be large enough to be a voice for local communities but not so large that it lost sight of national objectives.

2. We see the new constitution as a social contract between the people and the government.

When the Federalist Papers were being written, it was fashionable to talk about the social contract between citizens and governments. People envisioned the new constitution as a social contract between the people and the new federal government. In exchange for giving up some of their individual rights—and implicitly, privacy—the people empowered the government to act for the collective good. This collective good included protecting the nation from threats and preserving law and order.

Madison (Federalist 47) believed another feature of this contract should be a separation of powers in government, another popular idea during this time. He specifically cited the absence of separate but equal legislative, judiciary, and executive departments as a failing of the English system.

3. We must be realistic about the new government's security challenges.

The Federalists didn't want people dismissing their ideas as idealistic. They realistically acknowledged that every nation, whatever its form of government, had to be prepared to defend itself.

Hamilton (Federalist 8) reasoned that all nations find it desirable to trade with others. The buying and selling of goods increase nations' wealth and give rise to healthy economic competition. Unfortunately, such competition can turn ugly and lead to war.

In ancient Greece, citizens routinely acted as soldiers during times of conflict. But, the United States of America did not have such citizen warriors. It was populated by busy people pursuing commercial and agricultural interests. How should the new constitution address this practical problem?

Hamilton explained that such national security threats require us to talk seriously about standing armies to protect our interests. Such a step meant giving up some legislative power to the executive. Hamilton's immortal words describe this:

Safety from external danger is the most powerful director of national conduct . . . The violent destruction of life and property incident to war . . . will compel nations the most attached to liberty to resort for repose and security to institutions which . . . [tend] to destroy their civil and political rights. To be more safe, they . . . become willing to run the risk of being less free.

Hamilton's words ring true today. The Federalist debate brought forth a new government required to balance the collective good (e.g., national security) with individual rights (e.g., privacy). In chapter 6, we will see how national security threats induced the federal government to use heavier-handed surveillance—curtailing individual rights and privacy—during the twentieth and twenty-first centuries.

4. We need to be realistic about human nature.

Everybody loves to stick their noses in other people's business. It's human nature. It's also a violation of individual rights and personal privacy.

The Federalists were well aware of this. They understood that such leaked personal secrets could kindle disagreements and factionalism. Madison (Federalist 10) observed that the "most common and durable source of factions has been the various and unequal distribution of property." Some things never change.

So, how could the new government fairly assess an individual's wealth and apportion taxes? And how could the government do this without fueling the fires of factionalism and prurient human curiosity?

Madison (Federalist 51) famously concluded that the government had to protect individual rights (and privacy) by controlling itself:

If men were angels, no government would be necessary . . . In framing a government, . . . you much first enable the government to control the governed; in the next place oblige it to control itself. A dependence on the people is . . . the primary control on the government; but experience has taught mankind the necessity of auxiliary precautions.

These "auxiliary precautions" would become the checks and balances of our constitutional system of government.

5. We must acknowledge that revenue is essential to the new nation.

The Federalist authors were educated men. They knew that parliament's refusal to grant the king funding throughout most of the seventeenth century had led to civil war. Hamilton (Federalist 12) concluded that our new nation needed a reliable source of revenue to remain independent.

The new US Constitution would call for the House of Representatives to hold the purse strings of the new federal government. Madison (Federalist 58) observed, "This power over the purse may, in fact, be regarded as the most complete and effectual weapon with which any constitution can arm the immediate representatives of the people, for obtaining a redress of every grievance, and for carrying into effect every just and salutary measure."

6. We need to understand that a strong national government is essential.

The Federalists understood that the first US constitution had failed because it had granted insufficient powers to the federal government. Hamilton (Federalist 17) believed the government needed commerce, finance, negotiation, and war (national security) authorities to defend the nation from foreign and domestic threats and preserve the public peace.

The defense of the nation was foremost in everyone's mind. Since the people had entrusted the national government with the nation's safety, Hamilton (Federalist 23) argued that it should have "all the powers requisite to complete execution of its trust." That included the authority to fund, raise, train, equip, and direct its military.

Hamilton (Federalist 17) also argued that state governments should be responsible for criminal and civil justice as "guardian[s] of life and property." After all, he reasoned, local law enforcement had been responsible for keeping the peace since feudal times.

7. We need to lay the groundwork for the ongoing debate about a bill of rights.

Alexander Hamilton (Federalist 84) argued that the Constitution was a bill of rights. He saw a separate bill of rights as dangerous because it specified exceptions to power never formally given to the national government.

Hamilton argued that bills of rights had historically been agreements between kings and their subjects. In England, such agreements included the Magna Carta and the 1689 Bill of Rights. But in these united states, the people surrendered nothing and retained everything.

Hamilton would lose this argument, and the protection of individual rights—and privacy—would be incorporated as amendments to the Constitution.

The US Constitution

In 1787, a group of extraordinary men at the Constitutional Convention drafted a new document that became the foundation of the US Constitution. It was ratified by the required nine out of thirteen states the following year.

The Preamble of the Constitution sets the stage. It acknowledges several issues that people had seen debated in the Federalist Papers, providing a continuous thread from the old constitution (Articles of Confederation) to the new:

> We the People of the United States, in Order to form a more perfect Union, establish Justice, insure domestic Tranquility, provide for the common defence, promote the general Welfare, and secure the Blessings of Liberty to ourselves and our Posterity, do ordain and establish this Constitution for the United States of America.

The body of the Constitution describes the composition of the US government. It outlines three branches of government designed with checks and balances to ensure no single branch exercises too much power. In many ways, Congress is modeled on the English parliamentary tradition with its bicameral structure and legislative authorities, including control over raising and spending money. The judicial branch—the Supreme Court and all lower federal courts—determines whether a person accused of breaking the law is innocent or guilty. The executive branch includes all the remaining government employees that work for the president.

The Bill of Rights

Containing the first ten amendments to the Constitution, the Bill of Rights codifies Americans' individual rights and the underlying spirit of privacy. Lawyers today use the First, Third, Fourth, Fifth, and Ninth Amendments to make privacy arguments, as well as the Fourteenth Amendment added in 1868. We will examine these amendments to understand how privacy appears—implicitly—in each.

The First Amendment

Congress shall make no law respecting an establishment of religion, or prohibiting the free exercise thereof; or abridging the freedom of speech, or of the press; or the right of the people peaceably to assemble, and to petition the Government for a redress of grievances.

The First Amendment talks about the five private rights of the individual. These are freedom of religion, freedom of speech, freedom of the press, freedom to assemble peaceably, and freedom to petition the government for a redress of grievances. We will consider each of these five freedoms separately.

Freedom of Religion: Many immigrants came to the New World to practice their religion of choice—often a Protestant denomination—in a country where no national faith was mandated. Maryland's toleration of Catholicism stood as a testament to the colonial commitment to religious freedom. Immigrants must have also seen America as an attractive alternative to a war-torn Europe where religious conflicts between Catholics and non-Catholics continued to rage.

Freedom of Speech: The parliamentary right to freedom of speech appeared in the English Bill of Rights in 1689. The US version provided each citizen a private right to speak freely without fear of government recrimination.

Freedom of the Press: This right was a reaction to English licensing rules requiring the review and approval of all colonial publications before public release. In 1776, a Philadelphia press published Thomas Paine's *Common Sense,* a pamphlet calling for American independence from the tyrannical rule of Britain. People began seeing freedom of the press as an individual (and private) right to be used to hold the government accountable. Nearly 200 years later, Supreme Court Justice Hugo Black would summarize this idea by saying, "the press was to serve the governed, not the governors."

Freedom to Peaceably Assemble: In English law, any non-peaceful assembly that upset order in the kingdom (rioting) was subject to the full force of the law and its punishments. The English tried controlling discontent in the colonies by prohibiting all assembly.

Freedom to Petition: The right to petition goes back to the Magna Carta. The 1689 English Bill of Rights reiterated that "it is the right of the subjects to petition the king, and all commitments and persecutions for such petitioning are illegal." The Declaration of Independence used this model when it faulted King George for not hearing petitions from his New World subjects.

The Third Amendment

No Soldier shall, in time of peace be quartered in any house, without the consent of the Owner, nor in time of war, but in a manner to be prescribed by law.

As we've already seen, soldier quartering was an issue in the English Bill of Rights of 1689. Parliament violated this right in the colonies by passing the First Quartering Act in 1765 and the Second Quartering Act in 1774. These required the colonies to pay for or provide room and board to British soldiers in America. The colonists objected, arguing it was a tax for services they never wanted, but the king ignored their complaints. Implicit in the discussion was a right to have privacy in one's home (see next amendment).

The Fourth Amendment

The right of the people to be secure in their persons,

*houses, papers, and effects, against unreasonable
searches and seizures, shall not be violated, and no
Warrants shall issue, but upon probable cause, supported
by Oath or affirmation, and particularly describing the
place to be searched, and the persons or things to be
seized.*

The word "person" means your physical body. Your "person" has "personal effects." Personal effects can include the stuff in your pockets, gym bag, home, or car. You think of this stuff as your personal property, something you own and control. In modern times, personal property can extend to computers, their files, and information stored in cyberspace. The term "property" also includes any real estate you own or control. The Fourth Amendment protects your person and property, including "houses, papers, and effects."

When this amendment was written, the legal principle about a man's home being his castle was already well known. It had been penned in 1604 by Edward Coke, an English attorney general. His exact words were: The house of everyone is to him as his castle and fortress, as well as for his defence against injury and violence as for his repose.

Coke means that your home is your place of safety and rest. You have the right to enjoy its peace and quiet. There are laws again people breaking into it. Even the government cannot invade it except under specific circumstances. This expectation of privacy in your home is fundamental to the Fourth Amendment and underlies the Third Amendment.

The king had abridged this right for the colonists in the New World. The most famous example came from a 1761 court case in Massachusetts. The lawyer James Otis argued the Crown had had little or no justification for the writs (search warrants) used to search merchants' premises. He added that such writs violated Coke's my-home-is-my-castle principle and the individual's "inherent, inalienable, and indefeasible" rights. These rights went back to the Magna Carta.

The rest of the amendment says that the people have the right for their persons and property to be "secure . . . against unreasonable searches and seizures." The government cannot violate these rights unless it has a warrant issued under probable cause that describes the specific place to be searched and the persons or things to be seized. Again unspoken, the right to privacy in your home and business remains paramount.

The Fifth Amendment

No person shall be held to answer for a capital, or otherwise infamous crime, unless on a presentment or indictment of a Grand Jury, except in cases arising in the land or naval forces, or in the Militia, when in actual service in time of War or public danger; nor shall any person be subject for the same offence to be twice put in jeopardy of life or limb; nor shall be compelled in any criminal case to be a witness against himself, nor be deprived of life, liberty, or property, without due process of law; nor shall private property be taken for public use, without just compensation.

Doesn't "I'll take the Fifth" means I'm exercising my right to refuse to give evidence against myself during a trial?

This right is one dimension of the overall guarantee of due process in the Fifth Amendment. Due process ensures that all enumerated rights, rules, and procedures are followed to ensure fair judicial treatment of all individuals. As a private right of each citizen, it prevents the government from exercising abusive power against anyone. The origins of due process trace back to the Magna Carta.

The Ninth Amendment

The enumeration in the Constitution, of certain rights, shall not be construed to deny or disparage others retained by the people.

Alexander Hamilton might have inspired this amendment. While agreeing that people needed to keep their rights, Hamilton opposed a separate bill of rights. He was concerned that government would feel it could exercise any rights not explicitly listed in the Bill of Rights. The Ninth Amendment sought to close this loophole.

The Fourteenth Amendment

The United States adopted the Fourteen Amendment after the Civil War in 1868. It granted citizenship and equal protection under the law to all persons, including formerly enslaved people. The Fourteenth Amendment extended the Constitutional rights guaranteed in the Constitution to all citizens as governed by state law.

Conclusion

The expectation of a right to privacy existed long before the United States became a nation. It was a value inherited from our English constitutional history that goes as far back as the Magna Carta. When the New World colonists tried to exercise these privacy rights—in oral, written, and printed speech—the British repressed them. Protests about unwarranted British searches of colonists' private property went unredressed. Privacy became a never-ending source of conflict between the colonies and the British Empire, ultimately resolved only by American independence.

The word "privacy" may not appear explicitly in the US Bill of Rights, but its spirit is there. Privacy is essential to our democracy. The reserved private rights of the people limit the power that the government can exercise. If we let our privacy slip away, we lose that power to whoever took it. And the Privacy Pirates are eager to see that happen.

Chapter 4

Inventions that Shaped Privacy

"Hey, what's this? Who's First Best Security?" Mary walked into the living room with her head bent over a sheaf of papers.

"Beats me," said Scott as he looked up from his laptop. It was a typical Saturday afternoon, Scott working on his laptop—Scott was always working—Mary doing chores before her shift at the hospital, Alice doing homework, and Grandma Ruby napping in her big armchair.

"Well, you paid them," came the terse reply. "You paid them three hundred and nine bucks on the fifth of June, according to our bank statement."

Scott paused, his head to one side.

"I don't think I did, sweetness," he replied. "That name doesn't ring a bell at all."

"Check your emails," replied Mary. "You know how tight our budget was last month. We're about to be overdrawn at this point. You do realize how much Alice's tuition—"

"I know all about Alice's tuition. And the mortgage. Give me a second."

A minute of silence followed, punctuated only by the tapping of Scott's keyboard and the subtle rhythm of Aunt Ruby's breathing, still asleep in the armchair by the rear window.

"Wait," said Scott. "Here's something. June 4, three hundred and nine bucks and fifty cents. It's—wait, let's open this—it's an invoice from Netflix for membership. I guess I paid it."

"Netflix doesn't invoice. Check it again." Mary looked over

Scott's shoulder.

"It must be right, sweetheart. It's got our correct address, our names, the last four of our joint card, Alice's favorite—"

"You don't know how to check an email, do you, Dad?" came Alice's voice from the doorway. "And don't blame me for butting in. I could hear you guys all the way from my room."

Alice plonked herself next to Scott on the sofa, deftly pirated the laptop away from her father, and said, "Look." A few seconds went past with a flurry of key tapping, and her hands were a blur.

"If you think I can follow—" Scott began to protest.

"Just look," his daughter replied. "See? That's their real email address. Some gibberish thing at gmail.com. This isn't Netflix at all. These people are scammers."

"They had all our details," Scott protested. He was beginning to turn red.

"They do that," replied Alice briskly. "Face it, Dad. You got scammed."

"Only because certain daughters put all our private information out on social med—" Scott snapped.

"Hey." Alice frowned and stood up. "I don't even know the last four of your credit card. You did this. Or Mom did. But if my help around here isn't appreciat—"

"Stop it, all of you," came Grandma Ruby's voice from deep in the armchair. "You three got about as much common sense as a doorknob. People been fallin' for the same tricks for a hundred years."

"Mom," protested Mary. "I thought you were asleep."

"Not hardly. And I remember," continued Grandma Ruby, settling back into her armchair. The three other family members exchanged looks but also fell silent, drawn in despite themselves.

"Yes, I remember. Had to be about 1975, I'm guessin,' when my Norman was still alive, and we was young. Some salesman got all this information about us from the neighbors, then quick as you like, we get a mail order bill for some furniture and wouldn't you believe it, I write 'em a check, and Norm does too, and we send 'em two checks when we're livin' pay to pay and can't hardly afford rent and the boiled potatoes we was livin' on."

It was a long sentence, and the old lady took a moment to draw a breath. Alice saw her chance.

"Did you at least get the furniture?" she ventured.

"Hah!" Ruby glared at her granddaughter, then grinned. "What do you think, child?"

"I think you got robbed," said Alice slowly. "It's called scraping. They buy little bits of information, and then they put it all together. Everyone sells it, social media especially. Sorry Dad."

"We're probably all to blame. Except Grandma Ruby," interjected Mary in a frustrated voice. "And now these idiots have our details, and our credit card, all confirmed, and they can sell the information and charge us anytime they like."

"We'll have to cancel our credit card," said Scott immediately.

"No kidding," replied Mary, still sounding frustrated. "And do you know how much work that is? Do you know how many places we've registered our credit card for payments? The water, the power, the gas, car payments, registration, doctors, and on and on? And then fighting with the bank over any phony charges? It'll take days. I should send you a bill as the family bookkeeper."

"I'm sorry, sweetness," Scott replied. He took his laptop back from Alice, looked at the scam email and the underlying address data his daughter had exposed, and slumped in defeat.

Mary walked over to him and kissed him on the head. "I still love you," she offered.

"Beats me why," said Scott ruefully. "I guess lawyers don't know everything."

"Can we have that in writing?" Alice chimed in immediately. And then everybody laughed.

*   *   *   *   *

There's nothing like an intelligence career to show you how much information someone can recover from insignificant sources. Hollywood and TV producers get giddy about the super-secret world of codes and ciphers. But the unglamorous analysis of small scraps of openly available information reveals far more than any secret message. Alice's mom and dad have just learned this the hard way.

This chapter is about the history of electric communications. Inventions like the telegraph and then the telephone made it possible for people to communicate over vaster distances more quickly than ever before. Later, computers, cell phones, and the internet came along and turbocharged our communications. With each technological advance, individual privacy confronted new threats.

The Telegraph

Samuel F. B. Morse invented the telegraph in the United States, receiving his US patent in 1840. Morse demonstrated his new technology to Congress by sending a message across a 40-mile telegraph line between Washington and Baltimore on May 24, 1844. The modern era of communications had been born.

So, what was the telegraph? The telegraph had a metal key that transmitted a message across a wire. By pushing down on the key, you closed an electromagnetic circuit. That sent an electrical impulse down a wire to the other end, where another key received it. So how did this really work?

Someone came into the telegraph office with a message and paid to send it. The operator sent it by quickly clicking the metal key open and closed in patterns, which sounded like a series of metal-on-metal clicks at both ends. The information sent also included data about the sender and receiver, like the outside of a mailed envelope. The telegraph operator at the receiving end listened to the message and translated it back into text.

Then a messenger delivered the telegram to the intended recipient. Since signals faded out over long distances, there might have been additional telegraph operators who received and resent the message at in-between telegraph offices along the way. Anyone involved in the transmission or receipt of the telegram knew the private contents of the message. They also knew who sent it and who received it. Telegraph technology began to challenge people's assumptions about privacy.

Morse offered his patent rights to the US Government, which turned him down. He then created his own private telegraph company to make his invention a success. Morse began building telegraph lines from New York to Philadelphia, Boston, Buffalo, and further west. The first transcontinental telegraph was completed in 1861, revolutionizing how quickly people could share information across great distances. By 1865, a reliable telegraph cable linked the United States and Great Britain and began making money.

Banks and businesses adopted the telegraph. In 1867, the first stock "tickers" began telegraphically transmitting stock prices from the exchange on Wall Street. They had paper tapes that investors could read at the receiving end. The pace of the business world accelerated.

That included the illegal business world. Criminals used the new telegraph technology to cheat. Having tapped telegraph lines, they knew the outcomes of horse races before the betting houses. Such "insider information" allowed them to place bets on horses that had already won. The law had to catch up by making telegraph tapping illegal, and then the police had to enforce the new law. Everyone learned the telegraph endangered the privacy of communications in unexpected ways.

Morse invented a popular transmission code for telegraph messages. Morse code consisted of short signals (corresponding to a "dot" of one unit) and long signals (corresponding to a "dash" of three units). He designed his code so more frequently occurring letters were sent with shorter signals. For example, a single dot (one unit) represented the most frequent letter, E. Morse's design cleverly allowed telegraph operators to send messages efficiently.

Other such "compression" codes sprang up. Since telegraph companies charged more for longer messages, it was cheaper for consumers to send shorter messages. So, banks and businesses created codes to describe transactions (like "buy 100 bales of cotton" or "send $100") with fewer characters to reduce their costs. These banks and businesses were sending lots of telegrams each business day, so the savings for them would have been enormous.

Then there were the secret codes that allowed people to communicate privately. It was then common for young couples to communicate through newspapers using secret codes in classified ads. People adapted these codes for telegraph messages. After all, many telegraph company strangers would handle these messages between the sender and the recipient, and there was no guarantee of privacy. Banks and businesses also wanted their private business information to remain confidential, so using secret codes for their telegraphic communications made good sense. And, of course, the criminal element also desired to transmit information secretly to communicate with their accomplices and evade the law.

The telegraph spread to other parts of the world. Throughout most of Europe, each government owned and operated its country's telegraph service. European countries began establishing telegraph connections with other countries. Everybody had a different version of telegraph equipment and practices, which complicated interconnection. The countries finally formed an international body (today called the ITU or International Telecommunications Union) in 1865 to agree upon telegraph practices across Europe. While individual countries had tried to ban codes, the ITU rules now permitted them. In all countries, it remained acceptable for governments to intercept telegrams in the name of national security.

The telegraph allowed individuals, newspapers, and governments to communicate more quickly and efficiently than ever. In the New World, the telegraph spread—alongside the railroad—across the American continent, joining the eastern states to the Western frontier. People could order things from the Sears catalog and get them delivered by rail faster than previous generations could have imagined. And all they had to do was give up a little privacy.

The Telephone

Alexander Graham Bell was awarded US Patent No. 174,465 for the telephone on March 3, 1876. Bell's patent was called "Improvements in Telegraphy" and described the electrical transmission of "vocal and other sounds." Six months later, Bell demonstrated the first successful one-way telephone call across several miles using borrowed telegraph wires. By May 1877, Bell had rented his first telephone to a business.

Like the telegraph, the telephone grew, improved, and expanded across the United States. By helping create local telephone companies, Bell Telephone made telephone service available in local markets, including rural areas.

How did it work? The first telephone service relied on one wire at the sender and one at the receiver connected through the ground to complete the circuit. This connection was subject to interference by telegraph traffic and other things. Later, the service started using an entirely metal circuit to reduce interference.

With this problem solved, the next challenge was attenuation, the gradual weakening of sound over long distances. The use of copper (instead of iron) wire began addressing this problem. It reduced the attenuation enough to make long-distance service possible across the nearly 300 miles from New York to Boston in 1884.

The American Telephone and Telegraph Company (AT&T) was founded in 1885 to create the United States' first long-distance telephone network, a challenging and expensive undertaking. AT&T's president, Theodore N. Vail, knew he needed to make money. Still, he also wanted to provide the best telephone service to the most people at the lowest price. Vail concluded he would need to be the only competitor providing long-distance telephone services to meet these goals. He also knew that the United States government discouraged such monopolies except under exceptional circumstances, like providing a public good to a large part of the population.

Vail believed that these were exceptional circumstances. He dreamed of a long-distance telephone service that could benefit many Americans. The government was willing to indulge Vail's monopoly plan, but with rules. AT&T got its monopoly, but the government would set the prices for telephone services. Vail agreed.

The US government's tolerance for monopolies decreased in the early twentieth century. In 1912, three years after AT&T purchased Western Union (a telegraph company), the government began looking at an anti-monopoly (antitrust) complaint against AT&T. This would become a turning point for AT&T. To settle the complaint, AT&T agreed to several new government demands in 1913:

1. It had to sell Western Union and let it become an independent company again.
2. It could no longer buy up independent telephone companies without prior government approval.
3. It had to let independent phone companies provide long-distance service by connecting to the Bell system.

Meanwhile, Bell's telephone industry continued to come up with new capabilities. The 1912 invention of the repeater—a device that amplifies signals over long distances—would make transcontinental telephone service possible between New York and San Francisco in 1915. That same year, Bell engineers demonstrated that voice could be transmitted long-distance (250 miles) using wireless technology, setting the stage for wireless communications. The telephone had become a national necessity.

When World War I broke out in 1914, every major European telephone system was owned and operated by its country's government. Wartime demands persuaded the US government in 1918 to try running the US telephone system; this was a financial disaster. Bell got its telephone network back in 1919 with a $13 million operating deficit. The issue of government ownership of communications networks was dead in America. Commercial operators once again had access to the secrets people shared in electric communications.

A new application of wireless communications appeared after

World War I: broadcast radio. The first radio stations appeared in 1920. Radio commercials provided a novel source of revenue when interspersed with news, information, music, and other entertainment. As AT&T's influence grew in this industry, competitors began complaining to the government. This issue would be resolved in 1926 when AT&T got out of the radio broadcast business.

Telephone services improved during the 1920s. By 1927, trans-Atlantic telephone calls were possible between New York and London by radio. Bell Labs, a research laboratory for the telephone company, invented coaxial cable in 1929, making it possible to transmit more telephone calls across longer distances than ever before.

Congress passed a law to control the telephone industry in 1934. It was called the Federal Communications Act. This law created the Federal Communications Commission (FCC), which had the power to regulate the telephone industry. The FCC could investigate telephone companies and make and enforce rules for them to follow. It began an investigation of all telephone companies, and AT&T complied. The final report, issued shortly before World War II, set the mood for telephone regulation in the future.

Bell telephone devoted itself to America's war effort during World War II. It secretly designed and manufactured military equipment like radar systems. Bell's radar research would pave the way for microwave radio systems after the war.

Bell introduced other technologies after the war as well. The first mobile telephone service became commercially available in 1946, linking moving vehicles to the telephone network by radio. The first New York to Washington TV transmission by coaxial cable also occurred that year. In 1956, Bell Labs' research into undersea repeaters finally made trans-Atlantic telephony possible via undersea cable.

AT&T continued to support the defense of the United States after World War II. It became a key player in developing guided anti-aircraft capabilities and early-warning air-defense radar. AT&T developed the world's first active communications satellite, Telstar. It was launched and went into service in 1962. By the time the government forced AT&T to sell its interests in 1973, AT&T's communication satellite company (COMSAT) was carrying one-half of all international calls on its circuits.

And what about privacy on the telephone? Early telephone networks were not like today's telephone networks. Often, you would need to get a telephone operator to help you complete your call. And by 1950, three out of four residential telephones had to share a single "party line" because of network limitations. If you were on the party line, you could listen in on anyone else's telephone call who shared your party line. They could also eavesdrop on you. People accepted this as the price of the capability. By 1960, new technology reduced the number of party lines to about one in four, enhancing telephone users' privacy. Unfortunately, this increased privacy gave telephone abusers and stalkers more opportunities to harass individuals with less fear of being caught.

Beginning in the 1960s, the government started to demonopolize the telephone industry. In 1968, the FCC concluded that consumers could use their own equipment on the Bell network instead of the equipment the phone company leased to customers. In 1970, the FCC ruled that independent companies could compete against AT&T in the telephone marketplace to provide services and equipment.

In 1974, the government launched a substantial antitrust suit against AT&T, Western Union, Bell Labs, and all the Bell operating companies. To settle this legal action in 1982, AT&T agreed to divest its local operating companies and compete against others in the telephone market. It got to keep its long-distance services, research and development interests, and manufacturing capabilities. This divestiture took place on January 1, 1984.

Technological innovation continued. In 1977, AT&T installed the first fiber optic cable for commercial communications in Chicago. By 1988, AT&T had laid the first fiber optic submarine cable across the Atlantic, which could handle ten times more calls than copper cable. In 1994, AT&T completed its acquisition of McCaw Cellular Communications Incorporated, the largest wireless service provider in the US, and renamed it AT&T Wireless. And in 1996, the Telecommunications Act became law, promoting competition between local operating companies, long-distance companies, and cable companies.

The telephone shrank time and space even more than the telegraph had. It forever changed how people communicated, and it shaped our expectations for privacy in the future. You no longer had to go to the telegraph office and give your message to a stranger. But there could still be other people on the line, like an operator who assisted you in completing the call or the people who shared your party line. So, telephone calls might have seemed more private than telegraphy, but other privacy threats were creeping in.

The Digital Age

All the technology we have already discussed did not single-handedly get us to the internet, the personal computer, or the cellular smartphone. The age of electronics—our age—was yet to come.

One invention we have yet to mention is the transistor. Invented in 1947 at Bell Labs, the transistor was a semiconductor amplifier that could provide automatic switching at telephone exchanges. It replaced the old vacuum tubes that looked like skinny light bulbs. Vacuum tubes used too much power and created too much heat when used as amplifiers in telephone switches. The development of transistors made integrated circuits possible. It led to things like modern computers, communication satellites, and cellular telephones like the one that will create Alice's privacy problems. Three Bells Labs researchers shared the 1956 Nobel Prize in Physics for developing the transistor.

The internet began as the ARPANET, a project funded by the US Department of Defense to connect sixteen universities and research centers across the United States. ARPANET introduced packet switching, the automatic switching of data packets across complex networks using TCP/IP (transmission control protocol/internet protocol). It allowed one network to pass off packets to another. The networking of networks (inter-networking) blossomed in the 1990s, leading to the internet we know today.

The personal computer emerged in the 1970s. It became possible because of the use of semiconductor chips. The personal computer took off when manufacturers could put a computer's smartness on a single chip at a price people could afford. It built on many of the successes of Bell Labs during and after World War II.

The first personal computers were primitive and unfriendly. Only geeks could figure out how to work them. Over time, the software and interfaces improved, bringing things like MS Windows and browsers. Such things made interactions with the personal computer (and then the internet) more approachable to less technically inclined people. Personal computers continued to pack more computing power into smaller devices until the personal computer became portable.

The first cellular telephone system used in the United States was AMPS (Advanced Mobile Phone System). This first-generation cell phone (1G) used analog technology. It became tremendously successful after AT&T and Motorola introduced it in 1983 in Chicago. Within one year, 1G had 200,000 subscribers; after five years, it had two million users. The first digital cellular telephones became available in the late 1980s and early 1990s. These 2G phones used bandwidth more efficiently and could support many more users. Many technical advances since then made the modern smartphones we have today possible.

These technological wonders put the ability to sell, violate, exploit, and compromise your privacy in the hands of every individual. Today, anyone can violate your privacy in just milliseconds.

Conclusion

It's easy to see today how the telegraph and the telephone changed the world. These technologies connected people more quickly than ever before. Follow-on inventions—like the transistor, wireless, and fiber optic cable—created new markets, bringing about broadcast radio, personal computers, cellular telephones, and the internet. In another hundred years, others will be able to render final judgment on our civilization today.

Along the way, we've learned three important lessons. First, businesses will do just about anything to dominate their market. Alfred

Vail persuaded the government to grant him a monopoly so he could create a national telephone network out of nothingness.

Second, the government responds slowly and deliberately to aggressive business practices. Again and again, Bell squeezed competitors out of its markets. Again and again, the government let this behavior continue for years before intervening with anti-monopoly charges.

Third, new technologies pose creative challenges to privacy. Such challenges may be unexpected, unintentional, and unnoticed at first. People only slowly realize that adapting the technology requires them to give up some privacy. Personal privacy can get trampled along the way.

Today's Privacy Pirates have inherited this legacy. They seek to create international networks to make money. Our government responds slowly, and privacy continues to erode.

Chapter 5

Laws and Supreme Court Decisions that Shaped Communications Privacy

"Dad, will you sign this?" Alice walked into her father's study and placed her iPad on his desk.

"A petition?" replied her father, adjusting his glasses. "What for?"

"Privacy," replied Alice promptly. "You told me to research it, so I researched it. Now I'd like to do something about it."

"Hmm. Looks like you want to pretty much shut down the National Security Agency," her father said slowly. "Who's behind this petition, anyway? And is that what you really want?"

"Yes!" replied Alice firmly. "They snoop on everyone, they snoop on Americans, they invade everybody's privacy, and all of you sit there and worry about me and Faceb—"

"Is that really the mission of NSA, though?" her father replied. "It's not really. In fact, they're really concerned about foreign governments and—"

"It's okay." Alice put up a hand as if to staunch the flow of her father's immense stupidity. "I never really thought you'd sign anyway. You don't want to believe that most establishment authoritarianism is about invading the rights of the disadvantaged and exploiting—"

"Poppycock," came Grandma Ruby's voice from the study door. She limped into the room, grabbed the iPad—for Ruby, invitations were something that happened to other people—and looked at the screen, unimpressed.

"You know, this used to be my study once," said Scott wistfully.

"People used to respect *my* privacy."

"Poppycock!" repeated Grandma Ruby, shaking her head, still fiddling with the iPad. "Commies! Who wrote this thing? How do I scroll down?"

"Granny . . . ," Alice looked at her father despairingly.

"Never you mind about your father," said Ruby menacingly. "People don't change. The sooner you learn that, girl, the fewer disappointments you'll have in life. You don't know who started that petition. Probably Commies. If you'd spend less time marching in the streets and more time—"

"Granny, I've never marched in the streets," sighed Alice, "and as a matter of fact, I *do* know who started that petition. My friends. And I thought your generation was all about civil liberties."

Grandma Ruby began to reply, but that was when Mary walked into the room, looking worried.

"Scottie, I need you. Privately. Something's happened. We need to talk."

"You look upset," replied Scott, full of sudden concern.

"I *am* upset. We need to get on this right now." Mary waved her iPhone at her husband.

"Oh, I see," replied Alice. "Secrets Granny and I are too immature to know about, huh?"

Mary looked angry for a moment, and then she suddenly slumped. "Okay," she replied. "You might as well all know. Everyone else does anyway." And with that, she handed her phone to Alice and sat on the edge of Scott's desk.

Alice took the phone with a put-upon air, but in a moment, the color drained from her face. "Oh my God," Alice said softly. She scrolled through a few more pictures. "I think I'm going to be sick."

Scott looked over her shoulder, then took the phone for himself. He looked at the pictures on the Facebook page and then half-collapsed into his armchair, suddenly an eighty-year-old man. Scott said nothing, just shaking his head. He looked as if he was going to cry.

"That's not me," said Alice in a wobbly voice. "Mom, Dad, that's really not me. I mean, it *is* me, but that's not my . . . real body. Somebody stuck my head onto those . . . those pictures."

Grandma Ruby looked at the phone, and her face darkened. "Devils," she said softly. "If my Norman was still alive, he'd shoot those asshats. And I'd help him."

"Dad . . . ," Alice said again, helplessly.

"Hotness at Hillcrest High," said her father, reading from the phone. "And here you are, or your head, on these . . . pictures, and here are your friends, and the right name for the school, and—my God—the beach where you like to hang out, our street, and these . . . these comments . . ."

"I'm really sorry, Dad," said Alice, now in tears. "Did I do this?"

"Yes," said her mother. "And no. It's just where we seem to be at. Privacy is a commodity, everyone posts everything, and no one cares until the day comes when they're the victim, I guess."

"People don't change," intoned Grandma Ruby softly. "I keep tellin' you young folks that. People don't change. An' now you know." She put a bony arm around Alice's shoulders and gave her a hug.

"Well, the hell with this," replied Scott angrily. "I am gonna do something. I'm calling the FBI. And the cops. And my congressman. We're gonna end this. Whoever they are, these boys are going to jail." And with that, Scott stormed out of the room.

Much later, Alice was sitting on the rear stoop, petting Muggs the dog, and looking out at their modest backyard. Grandma Ruby was sitting next to her, saying nothing. Ruby could be annoying much of the time, but at critical moments, she always seemed to know what to do.

Alice smiled.

"What's so funny, child?" said Ruby softly, hugging her granddaughter.

"All this time, I've been worried about the wrong privacy," replied Alice. "I was nervous about the government. And I should have been worried about businesses at least as much. Maybe more. All they want is to sell our privacy and make money."

"We live and learn, child," replied Grandma Ruby softly. "That is"—she tilted her head to one side and continued after a momentary pause—"if we're lucky."

*   *   *   *   *

Americans worried a lot less about the privacy of their communications before modern technologies came along. Life was simpler back then. The sender of a first-class letter sealed her message inside the envelope she addressed and expected its content to remain private. There was no reason for the post office to open it.

This tradition goes back to at least 1792 when the new United States passed a law to create its post office system. It was our first law that discussed privacy in communications. It gave letters a "privacy right" by introducing penalties for post office employees who opened any piece of mail. The Supreme Court reiterated this idea in 1878 when it said:

> Letters . . . are fully guarded against examination and inspection, except as to their outward form and weight, . . . The constitutional . . . right of the people to be secure in their papers against unreasonable searches and seizures extends to their papers, thus closed against inspection, wherever they may be. Whilst in the mail, they can only be opened and examined under . . . warrant . . .

Supreme Court Rulings on Communications Privacy

When the telegraph and telephone came along, federal law did . . . nothing. Eavesdroppers could listen in on messages by tapping the wired lines or intercepting the message in the air. The law enforcement community could get copies of telegrams from the telegraph companies— often without warrants—and use them as evidence in court. The absence of clear federal laws allowed local, state, and federal law enforcement to introduce intercepted telephone conversations as evidence in the courts until the middle of the century.

The Supreme Court of the United States (SCOTUS) finally waded into the communications privacy quagmire in the 1920s in *Olmstead v. United States*. Roy Olmstead had been convicted of bootlegging with wiretap evidence. Olmstead appealed the decision, his counsel arguing that the government had obtained the evidence illegally and, therefore, had violated his client's Fourth and Fifth Amendment rights.

The Supreme Court ruled that the evidence and wiretapping, in general, were legal. Chief Justice Taft wrote that the Fourth Amendment did not protect telegraph and telephone messages like it did sealed letters. The defendant's home had not been entered, and there had been no search and seizure.

Three justices, however, disagreed with this majority opinion. Justice Brandeis wrote the dissent.

Brandeis first noted that the law must evolve to remain relevant. He then talked about how the times had changed. Science had given the government new ways to invade privacy:

> Discovery and invention have made it possible for the Government, by means far more effective than stretching upon the rack, to obtain disclosure in court of what is whispered in the closet . . . The progress of science in furnishing the Government with means of espionage is not likely to stop with wiretapping. Ways may someday be developed by which the Government, without removing papers from secret drawers, can reproduce them in court, and by which it will be enabled to expose to a jury the most intimate occurrences of the home. Advances in the psychic and related sciences may bring means of exploring unexpressed beliefs, thoughts and emotions.

No, the internet hadn't been invented yet. Still, Brandeis already imagined a time when technology might threaten our privacy as it does today.

Brandeis then reminded his readers of the intent of our country's founders:

> The makers of our Constitution undertook to secure conditions favorable to the pursuit of happiness. They recognized the significance of man's spiritual nature, of his feelings, and of his intellect . . . They sought to protect Americans in their beliefs, their thoughts, their emotions, and their sensations. They conferred, as against the Government, the right to be let alone—the most comprehensive of rights, and the right most valued by civilized men. To protect that right, every unjustifiable intrusion by the Government upon the privacy of the individual, whatever the means employed, must be deemed a violation of the Fourth Amendment.

It took decades until the Supreme Court began consistently agreeing with Brandeis. In 1967, the court reversed its opinion about wiretapping in the case of *Katz v. United States*. Charles Katz had been convicted of gambling. The government had collected the evidence against him by wiretapping a telephone booth without a warrant. The Supreme Court decided this violated Katz's constitutional rights. Justice Stewart wrote:

> The Government's activities in electronically listening to and recording the petitioner's words violated the privacy upon which he justifiably relied while using the telephone booth, and thus constituted a "search and seizure" within the meaning of the Fourth Amendment. The fact that the electronic device employed to achieve that end did not happen to penetrate the wall of the booth can have no constitutional significance.

The conclusion in *Katz v. United States* was that "Wherever a man may be, he is entitled to know that he will remain free from unreasonable searches and seizures." Finally, greater privacy rights would start being extended to individuals using communications systems.

How Congress Weighed In

Congress had thought about privacy when it wrote the 1934 Communications Act discussed in the last chapter. Section 605 of this law prohibited anyone, besides the intended recipient, from receiving or transmitting any telephone or telegraph communication or sharing it. Exceptions were allowed under "lawful authority."

What was lawful authority? We will talk a lot about this later. For now, we can say that federal, state, and local government—including law enforcement—thought that lawful authority was whatever they wanted. They largely ignored section 605 because they believed wiretapping and eavesdropping were essential tools for catching crooks. Congressional interest in passing any clarifying legislation would wane during the buildup, duration, and aftermath of World War II.

Congress would finally settle this issue in 1968 with the Federal Wiretap Act. This law made unauthorized interception of wire and oral communications illegal for everyone, including the government. It required the government to obtain wiretapping warrants and defined when information from wiretaps could be shared and used. It also prohibited unauthorized interceptions from being used as evidence in any court. The law generically prohibited the interception and disclosure of wire and oral communications by electronic, mechanical, or other devices, capabilities we broadly refer to today as electronic surveillance.

Conclusion

The first-class letter created our first expectation for privacy in communications. New communications technologies like the telegraph and telephone were far less private. There was no sealed envelope around the electronic telegraphic message or the telephone conversation.

It took many decades for the Supreme Court to rule consistently in favor of individual rights over government and law enforcement concerns. Individual justices like Louis Brandeis saw the need for increased privacy protections early on. Still, it took until 1967 before a majority of Supreme Court justices consistently agreed with his thinking.

Congress acknowledged the privacy challenges posed by new technologies—modern communications systems—in the 1934 Communications Act. Section 605 prohibited surveillance of telegraph and telephone communications, but many government entities considered themselves exempt as lawful authorities. Congress did nothing to stop them until passing the 1968 Wiretap Act.

Congress left one loophole. This law could not be used to limit the president's constitutional power to do what was necessary to protect the nation from hostile acts or attacks. This presidential power continued to be leveraged for warrantless electronic surveillance. In the next chapter, we'll see how Congress eventually passed another law to address this. Unfortunately, these actions would not protect us from the machinations of today's Privacy Pirates.

Chapter 6

The Security Threats
that Shaped Privacy Law

Scott strode angrily into the kitchen and sat down. Mary was waiting at the kitchen table, watching, but she was too smart to say anything.

"Four hours!" yelled Scott, opening the fridge door and grabbing a Blue Moon. He offered the beer to Mary, who shook her head, and then twisted off the cap and took a long drink.

"Four hours!" he repeated, shaking his head.

"Well, what did you expect?"

"Service. Availability. A little respect. And I gave that guy money, too."

"You should have given him more," said Mary, with a slight grin.

"I wish you'd take me seriously." Scott sat at the kitchen table and took another hit from the beer.

"I'm serious," replied Mary. "You're a sweet man for trying." She leaned over to Scott and gave him a kiss. "But what did you expect from a congressman, though, really?"

"I wouldn't know. It took me an hour to get through to the voicemail of some arrogant kid who was about twelve. Then I finally got the voicemail of some other guy named Ellis McKay, who's his legislative affairs director."

"What did he say?"

"Beats me. His deputy assistant something-or-other called back.

And all she wanted to talk about was what the congressman is supposedly already doing about privacy protections. Sounded like nothing to me. And I told her Alice's story, and she interrupted me about five times and then couldn't remember our daughter's name."

"I'm sorry, sweetie. Did you do any better with the FBI?"

"Yes actually. I ended up with a very nice special agent named Roshonda Lewis."

"And?"

"And she said they couldn't do much unless a law had been broken. And she wasn't sure what law. And I said I wasn't either. There must be something, though, for God's sake. She's fourteen. And those boys used her image without her permission. And those porn postings gave up personal information and exposed her to risk from perverts. There must be something there."

"Where did you leave it?"

"She said she'd look into it. And that she'd talk to her boss as well and get back to me. But…"

"But what?"

"Also, that they get about two thousand calls like this a month. And that because these young people are posting stuff voluntarily, there's very little they can do unless there are other associated crimes. I think she was telling me not to get my hopes up."

"Sorry, sweetie. Stay on them. But at least the police responded."

"No, they didn't."

"Oh yes they did. Look out the window."

Two minutes later, officers Chan and Watson were seated at the kitchen table, listening attentively. Over many interruptions from the radios on their belts, they sat and took notes as Scott and Mary explained the whole story with Alice, her beach photos, and the doctored Facebook pictures.

Chan shook her head. "I'm really sorry this happened to you and your wife, sir," she said, sounding sincere. "Pretty much the same thing happened to my daughter."

"You're kidding," replied Mary, wide-eyed.

"Wish I was," responded Chan. "Lily's images got used for—well, for undesirable websites. Perfectly innocent images, just kids at the pool. Next thing you know, she's identified as a cop's daughter, and then, well, every political idiot—"

"There was nothing you could do? What did you do?" said Mary, clasping hands with Scott under the table.

"Nothing we could do. We thought about moving to save Lily from the other kids at school, but we both have county jobs. So, we stuck it out. And who do you arrest, even if there's a crime? These guys could be in Russia, or China, or anywhere. We just waited for it to blow over."

"Until the next victim comes along," said Scott darkly.

"Well . . . yes," Chan replied, "I'm very sorry this happened, sir," she repeated. "We'll definitely file a report. There's too much of this going on these days."

Scott and Mary thanked the two officers, and just like that, their options were exhausted.

The next day, Scott was in the office. He knocked on the door of Dan Standish, the managing partner of Garvey, Standish, and Smith, and was motioned in.

"Yes, Scott?" Dan radiated the same polite impatience he always radiated.

"Dan, sorry to bother you. But you're our top expert on privacy law, and I need your advice. It's personal, I'm afraid."

Dan visibly slowed, and suddenly the impatience was gone.

"If it's personal, then it's serious," said Dan gravely. "Tell me the whole story."

Scott did just that, not omitting his worries about the safety of his family and his dead ends with his congressman, the FBI, and the police.

Then there was a very long silence.

"Scott, you won't like my answer. Do you want the truth?"

"Yes."

"Okay. There's no movement on privacy because billions of dollars are at stake. Facebook and Twitter don't want any more rules to follow. It isn't an issue that gets politicians elected. And the lobbyists spend more in a day than the entire budget of this law firm for a year."

Scott sat dejectedly, digesting this update from one of the nation's top privacy lawyers.

"So, things are never going to change? It's never going to get better? Congress is never going to help us solve all the new issues with privacy?"

Dan Standish sat for another long moment and then shook his silvery head.

"Ask me again in twenty years," he replied.

*   *   *   *   *

We've all felt what Scott feels: technology is eating away at our privacy. And it is. Congress wrote the current laws long before these technologies came along and posed these unanticipated threats to privacy.

If we lived in a tyranny, our tyrant could change these laws whenever he wanted. We see that done in non-democratic nations every day. But that's not how things work in our democracy. In our democracy, the law evolves slowly by design.

Congress can't just change the law when a new technology appears. It must wait for the people to want change. Why?

The members of the House and Senate will not get re-elected if they change laws before their constituents want the changes. It can take years for a majority of a district's or state's voters to agree on anything. And then, the House must agree among its 435 members on a bill, and the Senate must agree among its 100 senators. If the House and Senate bills disagree, then Congress must reconcile them. The reconciled bill then goes to the president, who can sign it into law or veto it. The passage of new laws can take decades.

However, changes in the law can happen quickly when the nation's security is threatened. Such threats can occur during wartime and peacetime, jeopardizing US interests on American soil and abroad. They can involve foreign actors or American citizens and include things like violent demonstrations and epidemics.

9/11 is one example. On September 11, 2001, terrorists attacked our nation; nearly 3000 people died. We were horrified. We were terrified. And we were willing to give up some of the power we retained with our individual rights to empower the government to protect us.

In this chapter, we're going to talk about the balancing act the US government performed during the twentieth century when national and international events threatened the safety of our nation. The subplot involves a battle to preserve American values against foreign beliefs. Privacy is one of these values.

The posture different nations and societies take toward privacy deeply reflects their own internal values. It's not especially surprising that capitalist and Communist societies have entirely different approaches to privacy. For that reason, it's worth reflecting briefly on the differences between capitalism and democracy on the one hand, and Communism on the other. As we shall see, the spread of Communist thinking—both stateside and abroad—would play a tremendous role in the evolution of American privacy during the twentieth century and beyond.

US Values: Capitalism and Democracy

We have always had capitalism in the United States. Capitalism is an economic system where private individuals own the means of production, like factories and farms. Supply and demand control the production of goods and the distribution of wealth. Market forces are left free to self-regulate and maintain equilibrium.

Capitalism is fundamental to our democracy. It gives everyone a chance to pursue life, liberty, and happiness. Individuals can freely invent and create whatever they want and make money by selling it; no one will stop them. Capitalism is an essential element of the individuality we cherish.

Foreign Values: Communism Challenges Capitalism and Democracy

In the nineteenth century, the Industrial Revolution helped American capitalism. As we've already seen, the telegraph made the business world operate more quickly. The railroads made it possible to deliver goods across great distances faster. Industrial equipment powered by water, coal, and electricity made factories possible. The machines in the factories helped produce things in large volumes and brought employment.

No labor laws existed yet to protect people who worked in factories. Factory owners exploited their employees—both adults and children—by requiring them to work long hours for little pay under unsafe working conditions. Life was grim indeed if you were a factory worker.

The writings of Karl Marx, a European who opposed capitalism, became popular among these workers. Marxist thought inspired them to unify through labor organizations. These laborers began agitating for better working conditions and pay, initiating strikes, and sometimes acting out violently. Government fears about worker unrest began to build.

Marx accused business owners of being greedy capitalists who were indifferent to the workers' plight. He instead proffered an alternative: Communism. Communism is a political and economic system that wants all property and means of production—like mines, mills, and factories—to be owned by the people and administered by the state. In its purest form, Communism will permit the working class to overthrow all state and class structures, like democracy and capitalism.

Under Communism, privacy is easy to control. The government is entitled to everything. The people are entitled to nothing. There is no slow march toward privacy rules that are in step with today's technologies because Communist governments rule by decree—and the opinions of the individuals don't matter. Absent popular revolt, privacy is not an issue.

Communism does not support free elections, private property ownership, or for-profit markets. As an economic system, Communism is the opposite of capitalism. As a political system, Communism is the opposite of democracy. Overall, Communism is the antithesis of American capitalism and democracy.

Already concerned by the spread of labor unrest and Communism in America, US government anxieties grew when the 1917 Russian Revolution brought Communism to Russia. The Russian tsar was deposed, and he and his family were executed. To Russians, Communism appeared as an attractive alternative to imperial rule; to Americans, Communism looked like a cancer spreading everywhere.

The Rise of Anti-Foreigner Feelings in America

Americans were suspicious of foreigners even before World War I. Foreigners had immigrated to the United States in droves as unrest in Europe and Russia escalated. Many of those new to US shores found employment in unskilled labor positions and became sympathetic to Communist thinking.

World War I and the Russian Revolution heightened Americans' sensitivity toward foreigners. Wartime patriotism bred heightened suspicion toward anyone with a German heritage as a potential enemy spy (some were). The Russian Revolution further fueled the fire of fear toward suspected Communists in immigrant populations.

These xenophobic feelings continued to fester even after the conclusion of the war. In 1919 and 1920, America experienced its first Red Scare. Bombs exploded in several cities, and Attorney General Palmer arrested many immigrants; he believed they had brought Communist and anarchist thinking with them from abroad. He worked toward deporting them as quickly as possible, largely overlooking any civil rights to which they were entitled. Immigration quotas in 1921 and 1924 limited the number of "undesirable" immigrants allowed into the United States.

Adolf Hitler's Fascism replaced Communism as the most significant perceived American threat in the 1930s. Fascism is a dictatorial form of government where national goals and goods outweigh individual interests, including privacy. The American crusade against Communism faded further when the USSR joined the allies to beat Germany during World War II. Having soundly thrashed the Germans, the US and Soviet Union became enemies again.

So began the intense competition of the Cold War. While initially a war of ideologies, it became a war of competing technologies and territorial influence.

On the technology front, the US demonstrated the world's first atomic weapons in 1945; the Soviets tested their own four years later. It became clear that Russian spies had stolen secret information from America to "catch up" on the technology. The public trial and execution of atomic spies Julius and Ethel Rosenberg in the early 1950s refocused American fears on creeping Communism in the United States and abroad. This technological competition between democracy and Communism evolved into a "space race" after the Soviets put Sputnik—the first satellite—into orbit in 1957.

The 1917 Russian Revolution had first aroused American concerns about Communism's spreading territorial influence. These sentiments were renewed after World War II as the US and USSR engaged in military competitions worldwide.

Americans watched fearfully as Communism spread. In 1949, the Russian-supported Communists won the Chinese civil war against the US-supported nationalists. Communism had spread to China. In 1950, a Russian-supported North Korea invaded South Korea. The United States joined the South Korean side for the duration of the Korean War (1950-1953). At the war's conclusion, Korea was divided into a Communist North Korea and a democratic South Korea. During the Vietnam War (1954–1975), the Communists of North Vietnam fought against the democrats of South Vietnam. Russia and China backed the Communist Vietnamese against the American-supported South Vietnamese. At the end of the Vietnam War, all of Vietnam united under a Communist regime. Despite America's best efforts, another Communist sphere of influence had come into the world.

In response to the threat posed by spreading Communism, the US government continued wartime activities from World War II that curtailed individual rights and privacy. Congress was at the center of the maelstrom. It passed two laws, the 1950 Internal Security Act and the 1952 Immigration and Nationality Act, to keep Communists out of the United States, track Communists within the United States, and expedite the deportation of Communists from the United States. During the second Red Scare from 1950 to 1953, Senator Joseph McCarthy conducted hearings into alleged Communist influences in the US government. The House Un-American Activities Committee (HUAC) extended its investigations into Communist influence in Hollywood. Because of these activities, many citizens lost their reputations and their livelihoods. As Alexander Hamilton had predicted nearly two hundred years earlier, the American people tolerated less freedom—and less privacy—for more safety.

Citizens Lose Faith in Government

Americans began losing faith in their government. They understood the US had entered both the Korean and Vietnam wars to contain the spread of Communism. But these ideological wars hadn't brought victories on the battlefield. People had tolerated curtailed freedoms—and privacy—to grant government greater national security powers. Still, things didn't seem safer at home.

American democracy's prestige continued to wane while Communism continued to spread. Cuba's new dictator Fidel Castro sympathized with the Soviet Union's anti-American views. In the 1961 Bay of Pigs attack, the United States launched a failed invasion against Castro. In 1962, the US discovered evidence of Soviet ICBMs in Cuba. America spent thirteen feverish days negotiating their removal with the Russians. Many believe this was as close to nuclear war as we ever came.

The US civil rights movement of the 1950s and 1960s expressed the public's dissatisfaction with the government. The Supreme Court's 1954 *Brown v. Board of Education* decision—ruling that public school segregation violated the Fourteenth Amendment—sparked a massive resistance to integration in the South. The 1964 passage of the Civil Rights Act was a step forward. Still, protesters continued to agitate for black rights, women's rights, sexual rights, and peace instead of the Vietnam War. Assassinations of public figures, like John F. Kennedy and Martin Luther King Jr., and rioting in American cities showed the world that the US was a nation in turmoil.

Things would get worse before they got better. In 1971, the *New York Times* broke the Pentagon Papers story. These papers revealed how the government had misled the American public about US involvement and success in Vietnam. The following year, the *Washington Post*, the *New York Times*, and *Time* magazine published the first stories about the Watergate break-in. In 1973, citizens watched spellbound as televised Senate hearings explored how the Nixon administration had committed unauthorized surveillance, burglary, conspiracy, and other crimes. Nixon resigned, and the country was seized by constitutional crisis. Many Americans concluded that even the United States president didn't respect their privacy or the rule of law.

The Church Committee

Congress had to act. In 1975, the Senate created the Select Committee to Study Governmental Operations with Respect to Intelligence Activities, looking specifically at FBI, CIA, and NSA activities. Chaired by Senator Frank Church (D-ID), it became known as the Church Committee. The House created the Permanent Select Committee on Intelligence. Chaired by Representative Otis G. Pike (D-NY), it became known as the Pike Committee. Both committees would conclude that executive branch agencies had taken liberties with citizens' privacy.

The Church Committee dug into old records of the attorney general, the FBI, and other government agencies. Its investigations revealed a history of government responses to perceived internal threats, like German spies during the world wars and Communists during the Red Scares.

In the 1930s, President Roosevelt had asked the FBI to investigate subversive—particularly Communist and Fascist—activities in the United States. Later that decade, he tasked other government agencies with helping the FBI track all espionage and sabotage efforts in the country.

Somewhere in this murky history are some critical details. The first is the presidential practice of asking the attorney general to authorize each wiretap on suspected spies and saboteurs and to restrict the wiretaps as much as possible to non-citizens. Many attorney generals continued to interpret the 1934 Communications Act—which made it illegal to wiretap without a court-ordered warrant—as applying to everyone except the federal government. The federal government would inconsistently apply the law to its own surveillance methods for decades. This confusion persisted until Congress passed explicit wiretap laws in the 1960s and 1970s.

The second important detail is that many presidents, attorney generals, and the FBI had tried to keep Congress in the dark about what they were doing. During the Church and Pike committee hearings, Congress realized it had not been checking enough on intelligence activities in the executive branch. The House and the Senate filled this gap by each creating a permanent select committee on intelligence.

Third, Congressional actions supported these intelligence activities. For example, the 1938 Voorhis Act required the registration of individuals who were agents of a foreign power. The 1940 Smith (or Alien Registration) Act amended immigration law to streamline the detainment and deportation of aliens considered subversives. It also required registration and fingerprinting of all aliens seeking visas to enter the United States.

These laws supported the FBI's efforts to create watchlists of individuals it considered undesirable. The first such watchlist was the Custodial Detention List, a list of pro-Axis sympathizers within the United States. The FBI used this list to round up enemy sympathizers after the US entered World War II. Many of these people were interned for the duration of the war or deported. The FBI also kept tabs on lawful groups and citizens, passing information directly to the White House.

Hot war fears about national security persisted into the Cold War era, preventing individual privacy from being restored. After World War II, the FBI kept lists of potentially dangerous individuals considered

Communist sympathizers. By the 1960s, the FBI had broadened its investigations and lists to include Communists, private organizations like the NAACP, anti-war protesters, and civil rights groups.

Cold War fears persuaded the government to continue monitoring international communications—letters, telegrams, and telephone conversations—after World War II. The Church Committee found that the government had been illegally opening first-class mail within the United States from 1940 to 1973. No president, attorney general, or postmaster general had authorized these programs before they began.

The government continued monitoring telegraph traffic after the war until 1975. It negotiated with all three telegraph companies to get all international telegraph traffic entering, leaving, or passing through the United States. The companies agreed on the condition that the attorney general had ruled these activities legal. This program went forward, although no record of attorney general approval exists. Once again, individual rights and privacy took a back seat to national security authorities.

Of course, the FBI had wiretapped telephone communications for decades; the National Security Agency (NSA) targeted international communications from the early 1960s until 1973 using watchlists.

The conclusions of the Church Committee were broadly this:

1. A wartime mindset—driven by hot and cold wars—had motivated domestic intelligence activities.
2. These activities violated citizens' civil rights (and privacy). Since America was now preoccupied with civil rights, these violations seemed even more disgraceful than they would have during wartime.
3. Congress would now provide oversight of government intelligence activities.
4. Past presidents had exceeded their executive powers in authorizing surveillance. In the spirit of the Federalists, Congress reiterated: "Here, there is no sovereign who stands above the law."

Congress also cited modern technology's role in providing extraordinary powers to the government. Noting that NSA could now monitor any communications (telegrams, telephone calls), the report stated:

> NSA's potential to violate the privacy of American citizens is unmatched by any other intelligence agency. Furthermore, since the interception of electronic signals entails neither the installation of electronic surveillance devices nor the cooperation of private communications companies, the possibility that such interceptions will be undetected is enhanced.

The 1978 Foreign Intelligence Surveillance Act

The Church Committee Report raised several important issues about privacy and electronic surveillance against national security threats. Are the communications of a US citizen protected when she calls someone overseas? Does the citizen have to be suspected of being an agent of a foreign power? What if a US citizen abroad calls a citizen or non-citizen in the United States? The line between foreign threats and national security authorities had become hopelessly confounded with domestic threats and law enforcement authorities.

In response to these concerns, Congress passed the Foreign Intelligence Surveillance Act (FISA) in 1978. FISA authorized electronic surveillance for foreign intelligence information within the United States. It permitted the collection of communications of US citizens acting on behalf of a foreign power but carefully excluded all First Amendment activities as justifications for collection. Congress inserted this provision to prevent the watchlisting and targeting that had occurred in the past.

FISA permitted the president to authorize electronic surveillance with the attorney general's consent. Alternatively, a federal officer could prepare a FISA application, which had to be confirmed by a government executive official and approved by the attorney general and a special court. The act also established rules for using FISA information as evidence in legal proceedings to protect the defendant's civil rights. Congress oversaw the usage of FISA, requiring regular reports from the attorney general.

FISA was reminiscent of the 1968 Wiretap Act. While warrants issued under this previous law required probable cause of a particular offense, FISA court orders required probable cause that the individual was an agent of a foreign power.

FISA also authorized communications companies to assist "persons authorized by law to intercept wire or oral communications or to conduct electronic surveillance" in support of FISA. Of course, that collection now had to be sanctioned by a court order or the attorney general. The phrase "electronic surveillance" became the generic term for "wiretapping" and "eavesdropping."

Congress has amended FISA many times. When our nation's national security has been threatened, like after the 9/11 terrorist attacks, Congress has strengthened FISA. When the country was more focused on individual rights, Congress weakened FISA.

Conclusion

Threats to the homeland during the twentieth century encouraged the US government to exercise extra powers to protect the nation's security. The government used electronic surveillance freely, ignoring existing laws and infringing on the civil rights of individuals.

Everyone—Congress, the courts, and the executive branch—had different views on the line between using electronic surveillance and protecting individual rights. Public awareness about how technology was eating away at privacy came slowly. Congress finally responded to the technological threats to communications privacy with the 1968 Wiretap Law. Damning evidence revealed during Congressional investigations helped put FISA over the top.

Around the same time, Congress began considering privacy concerns associated with government computer systems. In the next chapter, we'll see how this discussion led to the Privacy Act.

Chapter 7

Congress Responds with the Privacy Act

"Mr. Kasongo?" Alice stood outside the open office door, wishing she could stop fidgeting.

"Yes, Alice?" came a deep voice from somewhere behind a stack of papers in the small office. "You have an appointment, yes?"

"No, Mr. Kasongo. Do I need to go to the office and . . ."

"No, no, come on in. I always have time for my best students." Kasongo emerged from behind a stack of papers and gave Alice a welcoming smile. "Dakar," he added, as he noticed Alice admiring a poster of a large city with a big blue bay in the background. "It's where I went to school."

"It's beautiful."

"Yes, it is. Now, what can I do for you, young lady?" Kasongo motioned to a rickety guest chair and returned to his own chair behind his desk. He went very still, and focused all his attention on Alice.

"Well, I kind of have a social studies question," she began tentatively.

"You've come to the right place."

"It's about privacy."

"Go on." Kasongo began to look really intrigued.

"I kind of took a bet with my father to figure out where privacy began in US law. He says it's not in the Bill of Rights. Or anywhere in the Constitution."

Kasongo chuckled softly and grinned at his student. "Your father the lawyer, yes?"

"Yes."

"Your father has been playing with you. He gave you a literal answer. But he wanted you to look beyond just the literal, I think."

"I don't follow."

"Here," replied Kasongo, reaching behind to a bookshelf, and selecting a small volume. "My personal copy. So please give it back. A complete copy of the Constitution and the Bill of Rights. Read through the Bill of Rights and tell me if the concept of privacy doesn't live between the lines there, in the ideas that made this wonderful country."

Alice took the book wordlessly, noting that it was full of annotations and had been read almost to tatters.

"The handbook for America," said Kasongo simply, motioning Alice out as the bell rang. "Also check out the article by Warren and Brandeis in the Harvard Law Review for, I think, 1890. It's all online. And now, get out of here and do some work. And . . . ," he added as Alice left, causing her to spin around.

"Yes, Mr. Kasongo?"

"Never forget what a wonderful country this is. And how lucky you are to live here."

Much later that day, and just before dinner, Alice dropped by her father's study.

"Dad, if I tell you something, are you going to lecture me?" She stood in the doorway, looking serious.

"Depends what about, beautiful girl." Her father smiled and looked up from his laptop.

"Just please don't say 'Well done!' or anything stupid, okay?"

"Okay."

"I'm thinking about going into the law."

Her father swiveled his chair so that the two of them were looking directly at each other.

"Honey," Scott said slowly, "Really, that's great. As long as it's what you really want. Don't let me push you into it."

"Well, the hundred-dollar Nike quest is helping," Alice grinned. "But no, it's more than that. Thank you for sending me to Hillcrest, by the way. We have some amazing teachers there."

"One day I'm going to find out what this is really about, right?" smiled Alice's father.

"Maybe," replied Alice with—if only she'd known it—her father's identical, matching smile.

Alice headed down the corridor to wash for dinner. Luckily, she didn't notice her mother and grandmother at the other end of the hall, conspiratorially leaning into each other after eavesdropping on the conversation between Alice and her father.

"Law school," muttered Mary pensively, as much to herself as to her mother.

"Oh, spare me. Who you kiddin'?" came the deafening reply from Grandma Ruby, echoing to every point of the mid-sized house. "I have known that young 'un since she was the size of a button. She was always gonna go to law school, from day one. Born talker, just like my Norman, bless his memory. Ain't just no earthly way to shut her up."

Ruby limped off to dinner, leaving Mary behind to try to stifle her laughter.

*   *   *   *   *

In our democracy, the governed have only given certain powers to the government. The Constitution carefully specifies limited powers to the judicial, executive, and legislative branches, with checks and balances between them.

The judiciary can't change the law because that's not their job. Their job is to interpret and uphold the existing law. They must observe the rules of due process and fairly judge each person accused of violating the law. If a person is found guilty, a judge sentences the violator with a suitable punishment. Court decisions (including the opinions judges write) reflect the spirit of the law and real-world applications of existing law, but they cannot change the law.

The executive branch cannot change the law. The president has many powers, like leading our country, commanding our armed forces, and signing Congressional bills into law or vetoing them. By himself, however, the president cannot change the law.

Only Congress can change the law. As we learned in the previous chapter, that change can be painstakingly slow. Our forefathers intended our lawmaking process to be slow and deliberate so that no faction could hijack it. It's not efficient, but of course, neither is democracy. Believers in democracy still see it as a superior choice over all the other forms of government. Winston Churchill, the prime minister that guided Great Britain through World War II, summed this up nicely in 1947 when he said:

> "Many forms of Government have been tried, and will be tried in this world of sin and woe. No one pretends that democracy is perfect or all-wise. Indeed it has been said that democracy is the worst form of Government except for all those other forms that have been tried from time to time . . ."

The Privacy Act

Congress began discussing a privacy law in the 1950s when the government started using computers to store citizens' information. It took its first step towards a privacy law in the mid-1960s with the Freedom of Information Act (FOIA). FOIA gave every US citizen the right to request access to information about him or herself in government records but made no provision for appealing denied requests.

In the middle of the swirl and scandal of the early 1970s, a call came to amend FOIA. Lawmakers responded aggressively with the 1974 Privacy Act.

In the act's introduction, Congress acknowledged that government use of computers could magnify the potential for harm to individual privacy. Misusing such technology could affect an individual's legal protections and employment opportunities. Congress even went so far as to say, "The right to privacy is a personal and fundamental right protected by the Constitution of the United States."

Congress wrote safeguards into this act to protect individuals from government intrusion. The Privacy Act gave each citizen the right to

- decide what personal information was collected, maintained, used, or shared;
- know the legal reason for collecting the information and how it would be used;
- be asked for consent before information was used or shared for any other purpose;
- get access to and correct private information in government records.

To accomplish this, the Privacy Act required government agencies to

- request and store only the minimal amount of information needed;
- perform accurate and complete record-keeping to ensure fair treatment to all;
- share no private information without consent;
- keep no records about a person's exercise of First Amendment rights;
- be legally liable for intentional violations of this law.

Overall, the act held federal agencies responsible for developing and following procedures that protected the confidentiality and security of the private data entrusted to them.

Fair Information Practices (FIPs)

The basic ideas in the Privacy Act came from a 1972 government report describing the importance of protecting citizens' private information. The report identified a list of essential practices that we today refer to as the Fair Information Practices (FIPs). Sometimes people call these the Fair Information Practice Principles (FIPPs), but they are the same thing. There are many versions of them, but they all come down to eight guiding principles:

1. Transparency: Each agency should be transparent and provide notice to individuals regarding its collection, use, sharing, and storage of personally identifiable information (PII).
2. Individual Participation: Each agency should involve the individual in the use of PII and seek consent for its collection, use, sharing, and storage. Each agency should also provide mechanisms for access, correction, and redress.
3. Purpose Specification: Each agency should articulate the reason for and intended use of the PII to be collected.
4. Data Minimization: Each agency should only collect the minimal amount of PII required for its purposes and only keep it long enough to fulfill these purposes.
5. Use Limitation: Each agency should use PII only for the purposes previously specified. PII should only be shared outside the department for purposes compatible with the purposes for which it was collected.
6. Data Quality and Integrity: Each agency should ensure that PII is accurate, relevant, timely, and complete.
7. Security: Each agency should protect PII with appropriate security safeguards against risks such as loss, unauthorized access or use, destruction, modification, or unintended or inappropriate disclosure.
8. Accountability and Auditing: Each agency should be accountable for complying with these principles, provide training to all employees who use PII, and audit the use of PII to demonstrate compliance.

While FIPs originated for US government use, you see them everywhere today. You see them in the online privacy agreements you sign before visiting a website. The ideas behind these principles appear in European privacy rules, like the General Data Protection Regulation

(GDPR). Truth be told, these principles underlie privacy practices in many governments and businesses worldwide. If you understand the FIPs, you understand the intentions of all privacy and security rules which have sprung up to govern PII in cyberspace.

As you can see, many protections limit how government can invade your privacy. They might not be perfect, but at least they exist. If only similarly strong protections existed to protect us from the Privacy Pirates.

Conclusion

The Privacy Act only applies to the US government. Because of the Privacy Act, the government must protect the private information of individuals to which it has access. It does not apply to companies and businesses that hold customers' private information.

FIPs were initially designed to apply to the privacy of individuals' information held by the US government. They today form a foundation for laws concerning the privacy and security of private information in specific US business sectors, as we are about to see in the next chapter.

Chapter 8

Privacy Law in the Commercial World

"Sweetheart?" Scott walked into the darkened bedroom. He could barely make out the form of his wife, sitting on her side of the bed, hunched over in the gloom.

"Sweetheart? Are you crying?" Scott sat next to his wife and reached for the bedside lamp.

"Yes. And don't tell Alice. Or my mother. And leave the light off."

"Of course," replied Scott, thinking quickly. "Sure. But what is it?"

"I'm going to quit," said Mary between sobs. "To hell with all of them. Screw them all. I'm done."

"Sweetheart . . ." offered Scott helplessly. "But . . . I mean . . . I thought you loved working at the hospital."

"Not anymore. They can all go and screw themselves. They questioned my professionalism!" she said, in a louder voice, before Scott could interrupt with another question. "They accused me of leaking information! After fifteen years!"

"You've lost me." Scott put a tentative arm around his wife.

"I'm supposed to have leaked private information about a drug trial," said Mary, nestling against Scott and still crying. "I'm suspended for possible ethics violations."

"That doesn't sound like you." Scott hugged his wife a little tighter.

"Westwood called for patient information. It's their drug, their trial. All the patient names and details were removed. It was just their test results, their own test, and Prue said it was okay, and I gave them their test results."

"Prue the supervisor," Scott said, gravely.

"That bitch. Then she denied everything, said I'd misunderstood her. And I did nothing wrong anyway. Nobody understands the privacy rules, so they all run for cover and blame the staff."

"Well . . . you have to clear your name." Scott looked even more serious.

"Thanks, Captain Obvious. I know that," came the reply. "But I'm not sure I care."

"Care about what?" came a high voice from the doorway, and a moment later, Grandma Ruby was in the master bedroom, her hand on her daughter's shoulder.

"Good grief, Ruby," Scott said, his voice rising. "This is our private bedroom. We need to have—"

"Ain't nothin' private from me if it's my daughter," replied Ruby. "I've known her longer than you have. And she's cryin.' So you're obviously not doin' much of a job, laddie buck."

"What's private?" Alice's voice this time. And in a moment, she was sitting on the bed too, cuddling up against her mother.

"Well, skin me. It's a convention." Scott smiled a little, despite his annoyance. "Mare, you might as well tell everyone and get it over with."

Mary did exactly that, and the little family sat in silence.

"Quit," said Alice after a while.

"Don't quit." Grandma Ruby was shaking her head firmly. "You fight, girl."

"Okay, but then let me help," responded Alice. "I did a lot of privacy research for Dad; you'd be surprised. And Dad, you'll help too, right?"

"Damn straight," replied Scott firmly.

"And I'll make a pot of tea. Maybe put somethin' in it," said Ruby. "Not for the girl, not for the girl," she added as she noticed Alice's parents' horrified looks. "Just for the grownups."

By midnight, with Alice acting as a very competent paralegal, she and her father had his study desk covered with books and notes. Ruby made three pots of tea in all, adding a generous splash of rum into her own cup at every chance and pretending she didn't see Mary's disapproving stare. Mary, for her part, rallied energetically, answering her husband's many questions about her workplace and who had said what to whom. By one a.m., their work was finished.

"I'll write you a note for school tomorrow—today—sweetie," said Scott, yawning.

"Don't be silly," replied Alice. "I've stayed up late before. I'm not a child."

"As you wish." Scott hugged his daughter and slid the result of all their work into a slim blue plastic folder. "Here," he said, handing the folder to Mary.

"So, I use this tomorrow," said Mary slowly. "At their stupid Board of Internal Inquiry."

"Since they won't let you have a lawyer at this kangaroo court, yes. And if they shaft you, come back to me, and I'll hire my own managing partner to turn these yokels inside out."

"I don't know, Scott. I'm not a lawyer. You think I'll be all right?" Mary looked worried.

"Sweetheart," replied Scott. "These people don't have a leg to stand on. They only think they do. This is office politics, not law. They don't understand privacy rules—which, to be fair, are a big fat mess—and so they think they can throw you under the bus. Just push back."

"Go get 'em, Mom," said Alice, and her eyes were like fire.

"Damn straight," added Ruby fiercely. "You stick it up them asshats in a place where only the doctor and the good Lord should ever look."

"Mom! Please! Stop cursing!" Mary looked at her mother and then back at Alice, mortified.

"That ain't cussin,'" replied Ruby with deep satisfaction. "If you think that was cussin,' then you ain't never heard cussin.' And now I'm an old woman, and I'm goin' to bed."

Fifteen minutes later, the entire house was dark and quiet. And perhaps somewhere on the other side of town, a hospital administrator tossed and turned in his bed, kept awake by an inexplicable sense of what was to come.

*   *   *   *   *

Mary's experience here illustrates how vague and confusing privacy rules are in the workplace. The Privacy Act can't help her because it only protects an individual's private information from government. So, what laws should protect individuals' privacy in non-government environments?

Congress asked this question in the 1970s. It created a commission to study the effects of computers and information systems on government and private organizations. The idea was to determine standards and procedures for protecting personal information. The commission concluded that Congress should not extend the Privacy Act to organizations outside the federal government. It gave four reasons for this opinion.

1. Free market competition will force companies to protect their customers' private information. Market forces will cause bad things to happen if customers realize that a company is exploiting their privacy. The companies will lose customers, face negative publicity, run up legal fees, and pay expensive government fines. The market makes it advantageous for all companies to follow FIPs.

2. The commercial world has more variability than the government. It is unlikely that there is a one-size-fits-all Privacy Act for the American commercial world like there is for the US government.

3. A requirement for the commercial world to subscribe to the Privacy Act would require the government to enforce the rules. To do this, the government would have more, not less, insight into individuals' private information. Such a requirement is not a good trade-off.
4. The Privacy Act protects individuals' constitutional rights, the rights citizens retain when dealing with the government, not industry. Applying the Privacy Act to the private sector could very well be unconstitutional.

The Sectoral Law Solution

Going back in history, we have never had one generic privacy law that applies to all businesses in the United States. Instead, US privacy law has historically been sectoral and remains so today. Sectoral means that we have specific laws that apply to particular sectors. In this chapter, we will look at the privacy provisions of sectoral laws in credit reporting, financial services, and medical providers.

Fair Credit Reporting Act (FCRA)

The 1950s introduction of commercial computers completely changed the American business landscape. Computers began collecting, storing, and sharing information across kludged-together tangles of equipment, cabling, and magnetic storage media. This primitive infrastructure supported the Credit Reporting Agency (CRA), a new type of business that tracked individuals' credit charges, payments, and indebtedness. Three CRAs today—TransUnion, Equifax, and Experian—still make the US credit world go around.

There were no rules on how CRAs should handle individuals' private information until Congress passed the Fair Credit Reporting Act (FCRA) in 1970. FCRA was the first federal information privacy law that applied to an entire business sector.

Congress' introductory words in FCRA acknowledged that the banking system relied on the fair and accurate credit reporting provided by CRAs. Congress noted that CRAs had to exercise this responsibility "with fairness, impartiality, and a respect for the consumer's right to privacy."

CRA reports might contain personal information about a "consumer's credit worthiness, credit standing, credit capacity, character, general reputation, personal characteristics, or mode of living." These were all things that could impact an individual's ability to get credit, insurance, or employment. We've already seen how the Privacy Act would echo these concerns.

FCRA limited the circumstances under which a CRA could prepare a credit report. The CRA now had to tell the consumer about report recipients and share information in the consumer's file with the consumer. FCRA introduced rules about keeping information up to date, investigating disputed information, and correcting inaccuracies.

Gramm-Leach-Bliley Act (GLBA)

Congress passed the Gramm-Leach-Bliley Act (GLBA) in 1999. It applied to financial institutions—like banks and credit card companies—and their customer relationships.

The GLBA privacy rule requires financial institutions to respect customers' privacy and protect the security and confidentiality of customers' nonpublic personal information (NPI). It also restricts the sharing of private customer information with third parties.

The GLBA security rule creates and enforces standards for financial institutions related to the security and confidentiality of customer information. It further specifies that fraudulent access to such customer information is prohibited and punishable with criminal penalties.

Health Insurance Portability and Accounting Act (HIPAA)

In 1996, Congress enacted the Health Insurance Portability and Accountability Act (HIPAA) to protect the privacy of individuals receiving health care services. HIPAA applied to the entire healthcare industry, including doctors, nurses, hospitals, medical insurance companies, medical laboratories, etc. HIPAA also included civil and criminal penalties for violations.

The HIPAA Privacy Rule specifies what qualifies as individually identifiable health information (IIHI) and how to protect it. It requires the healthcare industry to request, use, and disclose the "minimum necessary" information about the individual, restricting the sharing of IIHI to the patient and those involved in medical treatments. The healthcare provider must also apply safeguards to protect IIHI from inappropriate access, use, or disclosure. The Privacy Rule explicitly prohibits the use of IIHI for the marketing of health-related products or services.

You have experienced the notification part of the HIPAA Privacy Rule in your doctor's office. It informs you of the healthcare provider's privacy practices. The rule also gives you the right to review, get a copy, and amend your health records. You also have a right to control whether and how much IIHI is shared with others.

The HIPAA Security Rule applies to all IIHI created, received, maintained, or transmitted using electronic systems. Healthcare entities must ensure the confidentiality, integrity, and availability of such records and protect against threats to and unauthorized disclosures of IIHI. A considerable part of the security management process involves risk analysis.

Congress passed a second healthcare act in 2009 known as the Health Information Technology for Economic and Clinical Health (HITECH) Act. HITECH greased the skids for the United States to develop an electronic health information infrastructure to reduce healthcare costs and secure and protect each patient's health information.

Conclusion

This chapter reviewed some of the earliest federal information privacy laws for specific commercial sectors. Congress enacted FCRA because it understood that the misuse of private credit information could affect a citizen's ability to get credit, insurance, or employment. We now can see that FCRA helped pave the way for the Privacy Act in 1974.

Subsequent laws continued to clarify the individual rights of consumers. GLBA identified privacy as a priority, requiring financial institutions to protect the security, confidentiality, and integrity of customer records containing NPI and prohibit their unauthorized use. The HIPAA Privacy Rule defined what IIHI was and how to protect it. The HIPAA Security Rule required the protection of the confidentiality, integrity, and availability of such health information.

The collection of US privacy laws you've seen is a good start. However, they still don't protect your privacy from being profitably exploited in the wider world of the Privacy Pirates.

Chapter 9

You've Been Cyberized!

"Now, Mary, the first thing we want you to know is that this isn't any kind of trial or judicial proceeding—"

"Sure it is," replied Mary quickly and calmly. She was sitting in a windowless room at Springfield Health with four other serious-looking people gathered around a mid-sized conference table. The grey-haired man who had addressed Mary was Dr. Fielding, the Director of Operations.

"Mary . . . ," Fielding shook his head and looked slightly irritated. "We're not here to lay blame today, or to look for fault—"

"Sure you are," replied Mary. "And if I'm going to be treated this way, Dr. Fielding," she continued evenly, "then I'd like to be addressed by my formal title, please. Nurse Kerrigan."

"Okay," said a middle-aged woman after a short, tense silence. "Well, Mary . . . Nurse Kerrigan, we do have an issue with the release of some sensitive drug trial data to Westwood Pharma. It does seem to violate hospital privacy policy, and our understanding is that—"

"That I released it," finished Mary. "Don't be coy, Moira. You're the head lawyer; just say it. You think I violated hospital guidelines by releasing drug trial stats to the same company that did the actual drug trials. Releasing their own data to them. Right?"

"Mary . . . Nurse Kerrigan," interjected Fielding, "Westwood is in trouble too. They should have clarified the government privacy rules before asking for the data. Even though they're arguing—"

"That I'm a signatory to their corporate policy for the drug trials and should have followed their corporate risk mitigation guidelines. Right?" finished Mary. She fished a slim blue plastic folder from her large bag and laid it on the desk, spreading out some papers. Everyone else in the room eyed the folder and the documents that now sat on the table.

"Mary, I know this is a difficult area," began Moira, trying not to look as if she was ogling to read Mary's documents upside down, "but our concern is for you and your welfare and what—"

"You couldn't care less about my welfare," replied Mary, still icy calm. "You care about your careers. And because nobody knows what the hell they're doing, the hospital blames the contractor for not understanding government privacy rules, and the contractor blames the hospital for not following their risk mitigation guidelines. And the workers get caught in the middle."

"You've certainly done a lot of research," ventured Moira carefully.

"Yes. I have. Does it surprise you that nurses can study and learn?" replied Mary sweetly.

"I think we've started on the wrong—," interrupted Fielding.

"And when we say big words like 'risk mitigation' and 'government policy' and 'caught in the middle,' it all sounds so much nicer than 'thrown under the bus' and 'workers get screwed,' doesn't it?" continued Mary, as though Fielding had never spoken.

"Now, Mary . . ." Fielding was unrecognizable from the confident bureaucrat of minutes earlier.

"You move against me on this debacle in even the slightest way," said Mary quietly as her eyes moved from person to person, "and I'll sue you all so hard that you'll lose not only your pants but your underwear." And her manner was calm and polite, and her voice was pure honey.

"Now, Mary . . . ," repeated Fielding nervously.

Hours later, Scott, Alice, and Grandma Ruby were sitting together in the living room of their cozy home, waiting for Mary to return from work. The shadows outside were growing long.

"Whatever happens, just be understanding," said Scott to the rest of his family.

"I bet she quits," replied Alice nervously, pulling at her hair.

A snort came from across the room, where Grandma Ruby sat in her big leather armchair, doing her usual impression of being fast asleep while, in fact, being wide awake.

"Something to add, Ruby?" ventured Scott with a slight smile.

"Worry warts. All of you. Worry warts. Y'all look like cats in a room fulla rockin' chairs. Sit down. Have some tea. My Mary's tougher than she looks."

"I dunno, Grandma," replied Alice, shaking her head. "Privacy rules are complicated. They're still evolving. It's easy to get trapped, like I did. People aren't very well protected."

"Hark at the child." Scott smiled and shook his head. "She's an expert, now."

"I'm right, though," replied Alice firmly.

"You are," Scott nodded. "And Ruby, I do think I'll take some tea now."

As Grandma Ruby was pouring the tea, they heard the key in the door, and everyone froze. There was a sound of belongings being dropped in the hall, and then Mary emerged into the living room, still wearing hospital scrubs.

"Is that tea?" she asked. A long minute passed as Mary, grave-faced, poured the tea and added milk and sugar.

"C'mon, Mare," said Scott, looking at his wife imploringly.

With a face like an Easter Island statue, Mary sat on the sofa next to Alice. Then she broke into a broad grin.

"They apologized," she beamed. "They actually apologized to me. I'm fully reinstated, my record is clean, and they promised me a bonus. You guys and your research are amazing."

And with that, she kissed both Scott and Alice on the forehead and then sat down again.

"Told you," said Grandma Ruby, with what could only be described as a cackle. "Just like the fairground when I was a girl. Round and round and round she goes, and where she stops, nobody knows. That's what the man on the big spinnin' wheel used to say. When nobody knows what they're doin,' that big ole wheel just goes round and round. Nothin' ever changes."

"Well," said Alice after a thoughtful silence, "At least the wheel landed on Mom's lucky number."

In front of an embarrassed-looking Mary, the rest of the family broke into applause.

*   *   *   *   *

Welcome to the brave new world of the twenty-first century. We have smartphones and computers that instantly send and receive texts and email messages. We use social media to post news about ourselves and to read that of others. Such tools help us feel close to our friends and families, even if we only see them for holidays. This new level of connectedness has changed our relationships with individuals.

It has also changed our relationships with the business world. Many of us now shop in cyberspace instead of driving to the store. The internet allows us to browse vendors' websites, select and pay for products, and arrange delivery to our doorsteps. Without leaving the comfort of your home, you can buy antiques from Europe, order medicines from New Zealand, and get silk shirts from China.

Cyber Vulnerabilities

But with the good comes the bad. The internet gives us some remarkable capabilities, but it also introduces vulnerabilities. The daily news reports how criminals use cyber vulnerabilities to rob banks, influence elections, and take advantage of individuals.

Ah ha! Now you're interested because these vulnerabilities could affect you personally!

There are many ways bad guys can commit crimes using the

internet. Most of us are familiar with hacking, phishing, and ransomware because we read about them in the news. More skillful attackers can defeat computer safeguards and steal personally identifiable information (PII), valuable business information, and even intellectual property.

A cyber attacker has the upper hand because he only needs to defeat the system's security in one way. If he is skillful, he can act anonymously and freely. His intrusion may go unnoticed for a long time, and his identity may remain a mystery even after the intrusion has been detected. It's hard to take legal action against a phantom villain.

The defender has a much more challenging task. She needs to protect the entire computer system and all its information from the bad guys, a vast and impossible job. The best the computer security person can do is to manage the risks involved in running such systems. She does that by using firewalls, encrypting sensitive information, using software to detect unauthorized users, and many other things.

In baseball parlance, it boils down to this. While the successful cyber attacker can have a low batting average, the defender must always bat a thousand. Because of this *asymmetry*, the entire world now takes cyber-borne risks to computers and networks much more seriously.

US businesses began using formal strategies for managing risk after the stock market crashed in 1929. The government passed specific laws to ensure that such a financial disaster could never happen again. Government regulations implemented the provisions in these laws. For businesses, these regulations would translate into things like standard accounting and auditing principles.

The field of cyber security adopted these techniques to manage risks associated with its physical equipment—like computers and cables—and the information stored on it. Accountants (!) adapted the idea of their Generally Accepted Accounting Principles from the 1930s for privacy. Their Generally Accepted Privacy Principles (GAPP) first appeared in 2003. These principles look like first cousins of the Fair Information Practices (FIPs) we discussed earlier. Both government and industry started talking about cyber security and privacy frameworks. Such frameworks provide skeletons of essential elements for managing the associated security and privacy risks.

Pirate's Gold: Your Private Information

The internet also introduced many privacy vulnerabilities. Consider internet shopping for goods and services. Each time you contract to purchase something on the internet, a certain amount of information is required. Applicable banking and credit card laws protect some of your personal information, like your name, address, and financial details.

However, the Privacy Pirates—the Googles, Amazons, and Facebooks of the world—can deduce a lot from your information with their artificial intelligence (AI) engines. They can predict your income, house size, and kids' schools by combining your online data with publicly available information about zip codes and tax records.

The Privacy Pirates also have your buying history available. Take Amazon, for example. Amazon routinely pitches products that fit your established buying habits. You might not think twice about this, especially if it's an everyday product like toilet paper or soap. But suppose Amazon suggests a specific brand of toilet paper or soap you bought previously. Suspicious yet? They are using your past purchasing history on Amazon to predict when you need more of something. With the introduction of subscription services, this feedback loop becomes a self-licking ice cream cone. You need toilet paper, so you set up an Amazon subscription to deliver toilet paper each month. You adjust the frequency and amount sent until you have a just-in-time delivery—enough that you never run out, but not so much you have no place to store it. Now, you routinely rely on Amazon to deliver these consumable goods and don't even consider other vendors. Amazon may be bordering on monopolistic behavior, which our government discourages. For Amazon, it's all about making money.

Now let's talk about a less common everyday product. Suppose you once bought a book on sixteenth-century navigation in the Indian Ocean. Now, six years later, Amazon lets you know about a newly released book on sixteenth-century navigation from Europe to the Far East. That's starting to feel a little creepy, isn't it? Amazon remembers years ago that you bought one book on a subject, and now they think you'll be interested in a new book on a similar topic. How would you react? Would you be pleased or paranoid that they are trying to tell you what to read?

Such predictions come from behavioral profiling. Vendors align their sales pitches with the well-established psychological principle that future human behavior will resemble past behavior. This level of influence is subtle, invasive, and sinister. You thought you were exercising free will to read what you want, but Amazon is trying to tell you what to read. Amazon's goal here is, once again, to make money.

The truth is that the Privacy Pirates have an asymmetric power advantage over the consumer. Each pirate not only harvests information from your past transactions but may also share it with others. Such sharing was what was behind the uproar about Cambridge Analytica in 2018. Since before 2012, Facebook allowed Cambridge Analytica to access the data of up to 87 million Facebook users. This data was used to influence the outcome of the 2016 US election. Even today, it remains unclear whether the Russian government was secretly involved.

The Federal Trade Commission (FTC), a government regulator, stepped in and pushed back. Facebook paid harshly for its role in the Cambridge Analytica scandal, paying a record-setting $5 billion fine to the US government. Cambridge Analytica also paid harshly; it went into bankruptcy and shut down.

The FTC is today very active in reining in the Privacy Pirates. Since 1914, this commission has been responsible for preventing businesses from using unfair methods of competition and unfair or deceptive practices. Unfair methods of competition include acting like a monopoly. Unfair or deceptive practices include things like Facebook telling users it wouldn't share their private information and then sharing it with Cambridge Analytica.

Now let's talk about cookies. Who doesn't like cookies? Imagine you take a big bite into what you think is a chocolate chip cookie, and it turns out to be oatmeal raisin. If you're a chocoholic, you're going to be disappointed. Computer cookies are a bit like this. They sound like they should be delicious, but really, they're not.

Computer cookies are supposed to streamline your experiences in cyberspace. They save a little data about your login and trusted device so that if you navigate away from and back to a website, the information crumbs are still there. They can remember your device and restore the contents of your shopping cart. They can also allow their owners to track your browsing history.

You may think this is all done to benefit you, the consumer. Well, a little yes, but mostly NO. Yes, it does streamline your shopping experience, making it easier for you to leave a website and return to where you left off. It expedites shopping, so you don't give up in frustration when your computer crashes or the internet hiccups. But all this information also helps the company to which the cookies belong. With this information, they can creepily track you over time and influence your online behavior. They might encourage you to come back and buy a product you were looking at three days ago or pitch something completely new based on your past interests. They can also sell your information. After all, your privacy is just a commodity to them. The Privacy Pirates' bottom line is all about making money.

But even that is not the whole story. You have only informal transactional relationships with many service providers to which you pay no money. NO MONEY. Like Facebook or Google. You pay no money to use the social media services of Facebook. You pay no money to Google to search, sort, link, and display information from across the internet. Are Facebook and Google just nice guys?

NO. We've already talked about one way in which Facebook made money. They sold 87 million people's private data to somebody else. But there is another way that Privacy Pirates like Facebook and Google make money without charging you directly: advertising.

The founders of Google devised the Google search engine in the late 1990s. To make money with it, they launched an online advertising service. They've refined that service to deliver targeted ads to Google users. Google uses your past transactions—your private information, your web profile, and data from other sources—to serve up ads on which the advertisers hope you'll click.

There is a subtle issue here posing a wrinkle for the law. People using social media platforms and search engines are consumers, not paying customers. "Transactions" in cyberspace occur when someone reaches out from one place on the internet and touches another. This definition differs from the traditional one that implies money has changed hands. The government clarifies this distinction by using the term "consumer" (of potentially free things) instead of "customer" (of paid-for products and services) protection.

The Europeans Push Back

Privacy is an extremely sensitive issue in Europe. The Europeans remember how Nazis disregarded human rights and tried to exterminate non-Aryans. After the war, people vowed this would never happen again. In 1948, the United Nations passed its Universal Declaration of Human Rights. Article Twelve specifically called out a right to privacy, stating: "No one shall be subjected to arbitrary interference with his privacy, family, home, or correspondence, nor to attacks upon his honor and reputation. Everyone has the right to the protection of the law against such interference or attacks."

These feelings motivated the language of Europe's 2016 General Data Protection Regulation (GDPR). This regulation says that the "protection of natural persons in relation to the processing of personal data is a fundamental right." GDPR protects the private information of all European citizens. Period. GDPR recognizes the threats to privacy made possible by cyberspace and tries to account for them. It even includes a provision known as the right to be forgotten, which is the right for any person to have his or her data erased and no longer be processed.

GDPR is a radical departure from US privacy law. Sure, our laws protecting people's privacy from government intrusion—like the Privacy, Communications, and Wiretap Acts—are not inconsistent with GDPR. Where the disconnect occurs is in the business sector. US law protects privacy in only specific sectors. In contrast, GDPR protects all citizens' private information from all commercial entities, including the Privacy Pirates. Maybe the Europeans have the right idea.

Section 230: Social Media and Free Speech

Section 230 has become a controversial provision of the 1996 Communications Decency Act. It states, "No provider or user of an interactive computer service shall be treated as the publisher or speaker of any information provided by another information content provider." This provision means that social media platforms like Facebook and Twitter are not subject to the same rules as publishers.

Publishers produce things like books, newspapers, and magazines. They have editorial boards that deliberate about what they publish. They subscribe to a guiding principle of truthfulness that they can use as a defense when sued for libel or defamation. With that said, publishers can reflect the editorial board's political leanings. Overall, the editorial board is responsible for the legality of their publication, and therefore they can censor its contents.

Social media companies like Facebook (now Meta) and Twitter (now X) are not publishers because their users control the content on their pages. Section 230 gives the companies a get-out-of-jail-free card; they cannot be held responsible for the content on their platforms. Unlike publishers, these companies cannot be sued for libel or defamation.

But now, social media companies have started censoring content put up by individuals. Does that make them publishers? Many, including members of Congress, are asking whether such companies should continue to be eligible for the protections of Section 230.

Some people have mistaken this situation for a First Amendment issue. It's not. Amendments to the Constitution only protect freedom of speech and freedom of the press from government censorship. Publishers routinely censor free speech in their publications. And now, so do social media platforms.

Mainstream newspapers and magazines in democracies publish factual accounts of news. Social media platforms do not subscribe to these publishing standards. They allow disinformation and misinformation to be posted at will and censor the posted content however they want. Isn't it time to start treating social media providers more like the publishers they have become?

Spin and the Information Echo Chamber

All information lives somewhere on the spectrum of truthfulness to falsehood. We can gauge its reliability by asking ourselves about the author's intent in putting that information out there. Words associated with such intent can include spin, propaganda, misinformation, disinformation, and censorship.

Webster's dictionary defines spin as "a special point of view, emphasis, or interpretation presented for the purpose of influencing opinion." A liberal newspaper puts a liberal spin on its reporting. As a publication, it doesn't lie. However, it might emphasize facts that make liberals look good and conservatives look bad.

Webster's defines propaganda as "ideas, facts, or allegations spread deliberately to further one's cause or to damage an opposing cause." A government can spread wartime propaganda to encourage its population or demoralize its opponent. It can be factually accurate, but its message comes with a spin. During wartime, people applaud propaganda that targets opponents, tolerate propaganda spread by their government for their benefit, and express anger about propaganda spread by their enemies. In this sense, during wartime, propaganda can have a positive connotation (sticking it to the bad guys!), a negative connotation (how dare they!), and all the nuances in between.

During peacetime, the word "propaganda" always has a negative connotation. As something that someone does to someone else, it feels deceitful and manipulative. Some might argue that the Privacy Pirates' advertising techniques, which leverage people's private information, are a hair's breadth away from propaganda.

Misinformation is "incorrect or misleading information," according to Webster's. Here's an example. Suppose you accuse me of lying, and I use the defense, "I was misinformed." I'm claiming that I thought the information was accurate; I never intended to mislead you. The subtext of what I am saying is, "Hey, don't blame me; I'm also a victim here." If my feelings are sincere, I could add, "I'm sorry for the misunderstanding."

Disinformation is more sinister. Webster's defines disinformation as "false information deliberately and often covertly spread (as by the planting of rumors) . . . to influence public opinion or obscure the truth." These are lies spread with the intent of supporting a goal. Adolf Hitler is a famous example of a dictator who undertook a massive disinformation campaign to spread his anti-Semitic views during the 1930s and 1940s. Today's internet is the ideal way to spread disinformation across the world's population.

Webster's defines censorship as examining written or oral materials "to suppress or delete anything considered objectionable." Again, the nuance associated with censorship is slightly different in wartime versus peacetime. The United States enacted censorship during wartime for fear that letters or telephone calls might betray valuable information to an eavesdropping enemy. The population tolerated it as a necessary evil. In peacetime, Americans characterize government censorship as a gag on First Amendment rights.

Don't get me wrong. Censorship on the internet is already abundant. Without it, the internet would look like a sewer and be far less useful. There would be lots of unsavory material that most of us would find offensive.

So, while you are free to post whatever you want, a company like Facebook may censor it. If you post something breaking US laws, you should expect government censorship. And perhaps a knock at your door. If it's criminal, you may even end up in jail.

Studies of human behavior confirm that people seek out opinions that confirm their biases. Everyone has biases. I prefer conservative politics, math over biology, and non-fiction over fiction. I read conservative publications, articles of mathematical interest, and books on history. But I also read liberal publications, articles about non-math things, and novels. I do that because I want to understand other people and their views. It helps me develop empathy toward others. I also do it because I want to be informed by more than just spin. I'm looking for facts and different perspectives to derive informed opinions of my own.

So, beware. Biased information creates echo chambers across our society. People are targeting your vote, time, money, or support by spinning persuasive arguments with partial truths and bald-faced lies.

Mass Media and Factionalism

The internet unleashed the most powerful mass media tool ever devised. It grants powers of persuasion that would make any despotic ruler weep with joy. And anyone can use it.

People who share interests or views find like-minded individuals via the mass media on the internet. Connectivity permits them to form groups that talk, listen, and share. Unfortunately, some groups develop extreme views and condemn all others. They become unwilling to validate, listen to, or discuss other people's perspectives. Such groups vigorously exercise their right to self-expression but seek to deny it to others.

James Madison (Federalist 10) identified people who share the same opinions as members of a faction, "united and actuated by some common impulse of passion, or of interest, adverse to the rights of other citizens, or to the permanent and aggregate interests of the community." As he weighed the pluses and minuses of a republic versus a democracy, Madison concluded that a republic would better control factionalism than a democracy.

Sadly, America today is less a nation unified around national aims than an unhappy confederation of factions. We've forgotten the social contract—our Constitution—that unifies us as a republic. This forgetfulness weakens our nation.

As members of a republic, we US citizens have the privilege of participatory government. With that comes obligations. We select our own representatives and hold them accountable through regular elections. In between elections, we provide feedback by contacting their offices. If our representatives aren't listening, we are within our rights to petition the government or protest peacefully.

We have civic responsibilities. When we go to the polls to elect our representatives, we must go as well-informed citizens. We must seek out the facts on issues and candidates, not just reassuring messages from the echo chambers we favor. Voting is both a privilege and a responsibility, and we shouldn't let others manipulate our votes for their ends.

Conclusion

The internet has transformed our world. Our cell phones give us incredible powers, but they pose sinister threats to privacy. Bad guys can use the asymmetry of cyberspace to exploit our infrastructure and private information. Risk management is a tried-and-true tool that has been adapted for cyber defense. People weave tangled webs of half-truths and lies to persuade us to click on ads, subscribe to news feeds, buy products, or vote for candidates. They seek to influence our behavior by appealing to our biases and emotions. Our private information remains a treasure chest from which the Privacy Pirates can collect gold. This booty grants them incredible powers. What can we do to protect ourselves and our privacy?

Chapter 10

Shoppers and Surfers, Beware!

"Is this a special occasion, folks?"

Zuri, the young server—she couldn't have been more than nineteen—stood in front of the seated family, grinning winningly, and waited for her answer.

"Birthday," replied Scott, nodding toward Grandma Ruby. "She's 75 today."

"Well, thanks for choosing Leitner's," the young waitress chirped. "Now, can I get you folks some menus and some drinks to start with?"

"Sure," said Scott, "I'll have a Coke." Alice asked for an orange juice, Mary also asked for a Coke, and Grandma Ruby—after a long look from her daughter—put down the bar menu with a sigh and asked for a pot of tea.

"Oh, and ma'am?" the waitress continued. "Congratulations on being 75!"

Ruby shrugged. "Didn't do nothin' but get old," she offered. "Ain't nothin' but time, that's no achievement. Time and the arthy-ritis." Then she grinned. "But thanks, sweetie."

"Congratulations, Mom," said Mary, and they all clinked water glasses. "We'll all toast again when the drinks arrive."

"I love you, Grandma," added Alice. "You've been a big help these past few weeks. I feel like I started the whole thing with my Facebook pictures. I think I'm just a bad luck charm."

"Tosh, child," replied Grandma Ruby. "An' I'm just an old fool, I bin no use to you. You've grown. You did it all yourself."

Everybody chuckled, but then Scott shook his head. "We all see your wisdom, Ruby," he said, looking right into her eyes. "These privacy disasters have all been bad news lately. It seems like they all happened at once. You helped us through."

"*We* helped us through," said Alice, staring at her placemat. "We all helped each other."

"And what did you learn?" replied Scott immediately.

Mary shot Scott a look. "Come on, Scottie, we're having a birthday party."

"No, it's all right." Alice looked thoughtful. "I think what I learned is . . . well, don't post swimsuit photos and don't trust social media, of course, but I think the big message might be that . . . life is pretty lame if we don't have privacy. I thought it didn't matter. But it does."

"It's like a big old ship from the old days," interjected Grandma Ruby. "You're sailin' across the ocean, and you're hopin' for a good trip, and inside yon boat is everythin' you care about. But them seas, well, they can be rough."

"And full of pirates," added Mary.

"The Privacy Pirates!" Alice responded immediately, looking very pleased with herself.

"Exactly right," nodded Scott in approval. "Exactly right. The Privacy Pirates. I'm writing that down." He grabbed his iPhone and typed busily for a few seconds.

"I don't think a democracy can work without privacy," said Alice slowly. "I don't think we can live our lives if everything is open to abuse by everyone. You can't live with a hungry tiger. And you can't live with the Privacy Pirates doing whatever they want to make money."

"Where does that come from?" replied Scott. "I've heard it before."

"That bit about the Privacy Pirates? That was me." Alice grinned.

"No, silly, that bit about the tiger," came the reply.

"Winston Churchill, I think. From Mr. Kasongo's social studies class," Alice replied.

"Quite right, child, well done," interjected Grandma Ruby, nodding slowly.

"But what can we do?" said Mary. "We're just a middle-class American family."

"Plenty!" replied Alice and her father in unison, and they both laughed.

"Plenty," repeated Alice. "In fact, it's what ordinary people do that makes all the difference. Stop trusting information to social media—they are not your friend. Ask people why they need the information they ask for. Get some basic skills like checking the origin of emails. Read. Keep up with events and the latest scams. Report anything suspicious. And pester your congressman for more attention and better rules—no matter how much money they get from the Privacy Pirates."

"Amen," said Scott. "Nobody looks after you. You have to look after yourself."

"And knowledge is power," added Grandma Ruby, her folksy mannerisms all gone. "You think it's ever been any different? You think it was any easier in the Cold War? With them Rooshians spyin' on us left, right and center? You think Vietnam was fun? Ah, nope. It's like my Norman—bless his memory—used to say, though I reckon he stole it from somewhere. The price of freedom is eternal vigilance."

There was a long silence as the little family thought about Ruby's comments—it was her birthday, after all—and finally, Ruby herself broke the quiet.

"And now—Mary, don't you even think about arguin'—I'm gettin' a martini."

At that moment, Zuri arrived with the drinks and took their orders, including Grandma Ruby's martini. There were several minutes of disruption before they all had their corner of the restaurant to themselves again.

"It's like we were supposed to learn something these past weeks," said Mary carefully. "First, Alice with her phone and her room. Then you, Scott, with that fake invoice scam. Of course, Grandma Ruby with that mail fraud back in the day. And then me, with my job. We've all had privacy experiences lately, haven't we?"

"If you can call it that," Scott grumbled. "It's more like a privacy pain in the . . ."

"Scott!" Mary frowned and nodded toward Alice.

"Mom, It's okay. I'm not seven years old anymore. I already know all the words," grinned Alice.

"…ass," completed Scott. He took a deep swig from his Coke, and everybody laughed.

*   *   *   *   *

Your cell phone provides a path into the remarkable metaverse. It's also a portal of privacy peril. With each visit, you risk leaving behind crumbs of personal information others want to exploit.

The Privacy Pirates extract value from these crumbs using powerful computers. This value is insights about you. These insights allow the Privacy Pirates—and others they share them with—to bombard you with advertising that appeals to your unstated needs, wants, and desires. The more of these ads you click on, the more money the Privacy Pirates make.

Shame on them. And shame on us for letting the Privacy Pirates get the better of us and our democracy.

So, how do we go forward from this point? Is privacy still important? What changed to threaten it? Is privacy gone forever? Or can we restore it as a priority? How can we take it back from the Privacy Pirates? Let's see, in this last chapter, if we can find some answers to these questions.

Privacy is Essential to Democracy

Our country began as a noble experiment. Our forefathers wrote its constitution so cleverly that it today remains the world's longest-surviving written charter of government. It inspired the constitutions of many other countries.

Our government exists to serve us, its citizens. We give up some of our rights to empower it to act. In exchange, we expect it to "form a more perfect Union, establish Justice, ensure domestic Tranquility, provide for the common defence, promote the general Welfare, and secure the Blessings of Liberty . . ."

While the word "privacy" does not appear in the Constitution, its spirit lives among the blessings of liberty outlined in the Bill of Rights. Privacy is an essential element of democracy; its absence endangers the foundation of our nation.

New technologies brought new threats to individual rights. Congress couldn't pass new laws or amendments until constituents were entirely on board. It took the civil rights movement to raise public awareness about technological privacy issues before Congress could pass the Wiretapping and Electronic Surveillance Act.

We need to protect our privacy from all who try to exploit it. We've done a pretty good job protecting our private information from our government, but what about from the Privacy Pirates? Will we let them continue to make money off our precious privacy? No. We must stop everyone, including the Privacy Pirates, from undermining our privacy and weakening our democracy.

Technology Challenges Privacy

Inventions have been undermining privacy since Morse invented the telegraph. Each new communications technology introduces new challenges to our private lives. Things we're accustomed to being private do not necessarily remain private today, thanks to the Privacy Pirates.

For example, take Amazon. Amazon technology makes it easy to buy consumable goods like paper towels, find obscure books, and set up regular monthly deliveries. Time goes on. Amazon saves records from each transaction, which it uses to predict what customers might want to buy again from Amazon or anyone else. Is this information kept private, or do they sell it? Could it be given to the police?

Consider Facebook, a social media platform posing significant privacy challenges. Americans willingly share private information about themselves in this public space with no thought of privacy. Naïve kids post immodest images, making themselves targets for predators. People share the who-what-where-when-why-how of family vacations, never thinking that such information can give exploitable insights into their families, fortunes, and unattended homes. Facebook provides a gold mine of confidential family information that strangers can use to gain unwarranted trust.

Smart devices introduce new challenges. Americans readily adopt them into their homes and lives without thinking about privacy. They install Echo Dots with Alexa throughout their homes that monitor family conversations and activities 24 hours a day, seven days a week. They acquire smart refrigerators that detect how much beer they have or when they need milk. They install smart thermostats that collect enough information to predict when residents are home, out for the day, or have houseguests.

Undoubtedly, online shopping, social media, and smart devices have benefits. But they are also eroding our privacy. Do you really want Amazon to know you're thinking about getting pregnant by ordering an ovulation prediction kit online? Do you think Facebook should know enough about your private life to make money selling insights about it to others? How do you feel about them sharing it with the government? Do you really want hackers to use the energy usage information from your smart home to know when you're out so they can rob you?

But that's just today. Artificial intelligence (AI) promises to bring remarkable future advances. Genomic medications and smart cities may indeed treat cancer and reverse global warming. BUT (there's always a but) they will introduce privacy threats. You will have to share private biometric information (DNA) to take advantage of such tailored medications. How would you feel if this biometric information became available to the police and led to a false accusation of a crime? The utopia promised by smart cities may turn into your worst nightmare if the city monitors everything you produce or consume. Do you want to be told you used too much toilet paper last month or that you must drive 100 fewer miles next? Don't you want your personal choices to remain, well, private?

Privacy is Savable

If privacy were a patient, it would be in the intensive care unit. It's not dead, but it is life-threateningly ill, and we need everyone's support to help it recover.

Every day in every way, we should consider the privacy implications of the device or technology we're about to use. We're talking about our privacy here, a precious right for which many fought and died.

You probably know people who believe privacy is dead and are indifferent to its passing. With attitudes like that, they're right. Their privacy is dead. They don't believe in it, so it doesn't exist. They've buried their heads in the sand like ostriches and assume anything they can't see won't hurt them.

We know better. We believe in privacy and are willing to fight for it. If anyone disagrees with this, remember the words of the cultural anthropologist Margaret Mead, "Never doubt that a small group of thoughtful, committed people can change the world: indeed, it is the only thing that ever has."

Help me change the world. Help me insist on the privacy to which we are entitled.

What You Can Do to Reclaim Privacy

Here are ten easy steps for reclaiming your privacy.

1. Get informed.

You have already taken the first step by reading this book. You now understand where privacy comes from, why it's important, and how it's threatened. You've discovered that the issues are complicated and keep changing. You also know that you'll have to start being vigilant if you are serious about your privacy. You'll have to stop and think about the privacy threats posed by letting any technology or internet-powered service provider into your life.

Remember the Fair Information Practices (FIPs) of chapter seven. They explain how your private information needs to be protected in cyberspace (and real space). The FIPs help you understand the underlying intentions of all privacy and security rules which have sprung up to govern your private information in cyberspace (and real space).

2. Remain informed.

New technologies, vendors, service providers, and sales strategies emerge continuously in the marketplace. The commercial world is forever devising new ways to make money that skirt existing laws and regulations. They don't advertise this because it's not to their advantage. Instead, they tell you that they are making these changes for the customer's benefit. Hogwash. They're just using the old magician's trick of getting you to look elsewhere (Look! A puff of smoke!) while they perform their sleight-of-hand. Every change should leave you asking what this means for your privacy.

3. Inform others.

Congratulations, you now know far more about privacy than most Americans. Now, go out and challenge other people's assumptions about privacy. Those who tell you that privacy is dead are giving up too easily. They actually have more power than they think. Begin by explaining how essential privacy is to democracy; every patriotic American should believe in privacy. Your goal is to get them to doubt their dismissive beliefs and start rethinking their positions.

4. Develop your own opinions.

You have a private right to your own opinions and beliefs. But how can you have informed opinions about things when the internet bullies you with half-truths, misinformation, and disinformation? Where do you find facts?

All researchers learn about the different types of sources. Primary sources—accounts from firsthand witnesses—are considered the most authoritative. Secondary sources use information gleaned by someone from a primary source, while tertiary sources are things like encyclopedias. These guidelines for sourced research originated long ago but remain relevant in internet research today, with a few caveats.

The International Federation of Library Associations and Institutions (IFLA, *http://blogs.ifla.org/lpa/files/2017/01/How-to-Spot-Fake-News.pdf*) makes the following recommendations to detect fake news on the internet:

- **Consider the sources.** Look around the website to understand the mission of the organization and something about its points of contact.
- **Check the author.** Is he or she credible? A real person or a troll?
- **Check the date.** Old stories unrelated to recent news are not necessarily relevant.
- **Check your bias.** Could your personal beliefs be clouding your judgment?
- **Read beyond.** People use outrageous headlines to get clicks. What's the article about? What's the author's objective in writing it this way?
- **Check supporting sources.** Check the references. Are they real? Credible? Do they support the story your source is telling?
- **Is it a joke?** Is this intended as a serious piece of writing or satire showing the absurdity of something? What does the author have a reputation for writing?
- **Ask the experts**. Fact check using reliable websites, or ask a librarian for help.

5. Be civil.

What do I mean by civil? According to Webster's, civil means courteous and polite. It comes from the Latin word *civilis*, which means "of or affecting fellow citizens."

In these fraught times, many people close their ears to other people's opinions. They vigorously exercise their right to self-expression but seek to deny it to others. By shutting down the dialogue, people cause the issues to fester. It tears our society apart. It weakens our democracy.

Part of being a good American citizen is respecting the rights of others. That means discussing the issues, not shouting one another down. Each person is entitled to present his or her perspective but must also listen to others' perspectives attentively. Such discussions can be difficult, but they are invaluable to democracy. Allowing the people to have a voice in all issues, including how they are governed, may look like anarchy. Still, it's what we chose over the tyranny of a monarch. Madison said as much in Federalist 18.

When you discuss anything, like privacy, with others, be civil. Listen to the other person's perspectives. Really listen. Then state your case. Use reliable sources to make persuasive arguments. Find things on which you can agree. If nothing else, you both agree that you want to be American citizens and support the success of our country.

6. Work your cyberspace defense.

Having read this book, you are now much more aware of the dangers of sharing private information in cyberspace. Instead of just clicking yes or filling in all the information asked for, you're going to stop and think about it.

But that's not enough. You've got to work your cyberspace defense every day. You will never have zero cyberspace risk, but there are some things you can habitually do to improve your defensive posture.

There are all the usual things you're supposed to do related to passwords, virus scanning, and keeping your software up to date. You probably get email notifications every day about this. You need to pay attention to them. But you also need to make sure they are from reliable sources. Don't click until you're sure you trust the source!

There are many guides to good cybersecurity practices. US government websites host many reliable sources. Type in ".gov resources for protecting my computer." After you skip over the ads (!), you'll get many US government sites designed to help you. Check out, for example, the CISA, FBI, DHS, and FEMA websites.

7. Insist on consumer privacy.

The commercial world prioritizes privacy only when the government requires it. The Privacy Pirates will continue to behave no better than digital totalitarians without new laws designed for the internet age.

The Federal Trade Commission (FTC) leads the way in reestablishing privacy for consumers. Go to its website and learn about what it is doing and its services. You can register a complaint with the FTC when a company does something genuinely appalling. Indirectly, such actions tell our lawmakers that they need to strengthen personal privacy laws.

8. Get involved with the privacy community.

An active privacy community exists in the United States with which you can become involved. It includes non-profit organizations like the Electronic Frontier Foundation (EFF) and the Electronic Privacy Information Center (EPIC). EFF bills its mission as defending civil rights in the digital world. EPIC focuses on protecting privacy, freedom of expression, and democratic values in the information age. Other non-profits, like the Center for AI and Digital Policy (CAIDP), focus on privacy concerns driven by new technologies. CAIDP aims for a world where technology promotes broad social inclusion based on fundamental rights, democratic institutions, and the rule of law.

9. Refocus on non-government threats to privacy.

Our "inalienable" rights give us superpowers over the

government. These superpowers limit the power of government and protect democracy. Anything that threatens these superpowers threatens American democracy.

The Privacy Pirates have been stealing our superpowers. They perform non-consensual acts on our private information, using technology to collect, combine, transform, analyze, synthesize, share, and sell it. Are we going to fritter away the rights we fought for in a war of independence? Where is our bill of rights for cyberspace?

Instead of being preoccupied with conspiracy theories about the government, I'm suggesting we refocus on how the Privacy Pirates exploit our private information. Then get Congress to do something about it.

10. Hold Congress responsible for your privacy.

Tell Congress we need stronger privacy laws NOW. Our US laws today leave us vulnerable to privacy exploitation by the Privacy Pirates, weakening our democracy.

Many democratic nations believe that privacy is an inherent human right. Their bloody histories taught them that standing up for individual rights helped preserve democracy. America should modernize its privacy laws and ease the privacy disconnect with its democratic allies. The power of the people, the safety of nations, and the future of democracy depend on it.

One hundred years ago, radio was just emerging, telephony was increasingly common in people's homes, and the telegraph was old hat. Americans were just beginning to see how these technologies could compromise privacy.

One hundred years from now, what will people think about technology and privacy in our era? Their views will largely depend on whether we successfully preserved American privacy and democracy.

Long live privacy. Generations to come, and our own children, are depending on us.

Appendix

Reserved Words and Phrases from our Founding Fathers

Common Good: See General Welfare.

Democracy

Democracy is a form of government where the power is exercised by the people. James Madison distinguished a "democracy" from a "republic" in Federalist 14, based on classical definitions: "In a democracy, the people meet and exercise the government in person; in a republic, they assemble and administer it by their representatives and agents. A democracy, consequently, will be confined to a small spot. A republic may be extended over a large region."

Madison argued in Federalist 10 that a republican form of government was better for a large nation than a democratic one since government has to be representative of local communities but not so large that it loses sight of national objectives.

Today, people commonly speak about American democracy, but what is really meant is a republic.

Domestic Tranquility

According to the Preamble of the Constitution, one of the purposes of the new federal government was "to insure domestic tranquility." Article 4, Section 4 elaborated by authorizing the federal government to protect the states of the Union against foreign and domestic threats.

Today, people understand "domestic tranquility" more broadly as peace and order in the homeland, including by removing threats from American streets and communities.

Due Process

The right to due process is the right to be treated fairly and equally under the established rules and principles of law, including in court proceedings. The Fifth Amendment states that no one shall be "deprived of life, liberty, or property without due process of law." The Fourteenth Amendment (1868) extended this legal obligation to all states. The modern definition remains much the same as it was at our founding and in the English common law.

Freedom

Benjamin Franklin defined freedom as "not a gift bestowed upon us by other men, but a right that belongs to us by the laws of God and nature." Freedom empowers the individual to exercise inalienable rights that include life, liberty, and the pursuit of happiness. The Declaration of Independence, the Constitution, and the Bill of Rights are sometimes collectively referred to as the Charters of Freedom.

Freedom became a hot-button issue during the US civil rights movement. Minority populations (i.e., people who were not white heterosexual males) exercised their right to demand equal treatment under the law, in social settings, and for employment. People will continue to agitate for equal rights as long as inequalities remain since freedom is everyone's right.

Freedom of Assembly

The First Amendment recognizes the inalienable right of people to assemble peaceably to petition the government for a redress of grievances.

In 1875, the Supreme Court ruled that the right to assemble peaceably for any reason when "connected with the powers or the duties of the national government" is a guaranteed right of citizenship (*United States v. Cruikshank*). Such a right is today viewed as supporting a person's liberty to engage in non-political assembly and personal relationships (see Freedom of Association).

In 1937, the Supreme Court ruled that the right of peaceable assembly was connected to and as important as freedom of speech and freedom of the press (*DeJonge v. Oregon*). Today, freedom of assembly, petition, speech, and press, are often viewed as linked rights that are part of a broader freedom of expression.

Freedom of Association

Freedom of association does not explicitly appear in the First Amendment. After civil rights became a national priority in the 1950s and 1960s, the Supreme Court began ruling that freedom of association is part of the exercise of free speech, free assembly, and the right to petition.

Freedom of the Press

Freedom of the press is an explicit First Amendment right. It guarantees freedom for publishers—people that produce things like newspapers, magazines, and books—to publish any content they want without government restraint (but subject to libel laws). Our Founding Fathers believed that the open reporting and discussion of views—including those critical of the government— were essential to democracy.

Social media platforms like Facebook and Twitter have begun censoring user-generated content more vigorously in recent years. Congress has begun looking very carefully at the question of whether such censoring makes social-media platforms into publishers—i.e., whether they effectively "publish" others' work as their own work, rather than simply provide means for users to publish. If the platforms are eventually found to be publishers, this could strip them of existing legal protections for user platforms and subject them to (constitutionally limited) liability.

Freedom of Religion

The First Amendment guarantees the free exercise of any religion by any individual and prohibits the federal government from creating a national religion. Through the Fourteenth Amendment adopted after the Civil War, state governments are also required to respect these (and other) constitutional rights.

People often assume that our Founding Fathers meant only freedom of Christian religions, but that is incorrect. Washington, Jefferson, Adams, and Madison all bucked precedent by supporting a religiously neutral government. They agreed to extend freedom of religion to all faiths, including Judaism and Islam. This principle stands today.

Freedom from Search and Seizure

The Fourth Amendment ensures that people "be secure in their persons, houses, papers, and effects, against unreasonable searches and seizures." British authorities had routinely searched the colonists and their possessions for smuggled goods, thereby offending traditional British cultural understanding about liberty and personal inviolability. Our forefathers considered the British government's practice intolerable and banned it in the new republic.

Modern technologies challenged—and continue to challenge—the application of the Fourth Amendment. For example, the telegraph was the first technology that could be wiretapped. Since wiretapping was an entirely new practice, there was no specific law against it. People quickly began to see, however, that wiretapping could threaten the protections of the Fourth Amendment. Courts became concerned as well, and Congress eventually passed laws governing wiretaps. This legislative response could not be a one-off since communications—and ways to tap them—are always evolving. Congress must routinely reform the laws to safeguard constitutional rights that technical innovations would otherwise erode.

Freedom from Self-Incrimination

The Fifth Amendment states that no one is required to be a witness against himself or herself in a criminal case and allows a defendant to "Take the Fifth."

In the mid-twentieth century, the interpretation of this amendment broadened as a result of Supreme Court decisions. Now, the Fifth Amendment can be asserted by any witness (not just the defendant) in any trial (not just criminal ones). In civil cases, negative inferences can often be drawn against those who invoke the Fifth Amendment, but such inferences are forbidden in criminal cases, where the Fifth Amendment more directly applies.

Freedom of Speech

Freedom of speech and freedom of the press are both essential elements of the First Amendment's implicit guarantee of freedom of expression.

The Supreme Court tempered this freedom in *Schenck v. United States* (1919): "Words which . . . would [ordinarily] be . . . protected by the First Amendment may become subject to prohibition when of such a nature and used in such circumstances as to create a clear and present danger that they will bring about the substantive evils which Congress has a right to prevent." The danger at issue had been a printed and mailed circular intended to obstruct military recruiting during World War I. The Supreme Court has also repeatedly ruled that government may exercise prior restraint when the expression is intended to induce, incite, or produce lawlessness (*Brandenburg v. Ohio*, 1969).

General Welfare

The "general welfare" historically meant the citizens' health, peace, morality, and safety. A primary reason for the US Constitution's creation was "to promote the general welfare." The mandate conferred by the duty of safeguarding the general welfare gave Congress the authority to collect revenue in the form of "taxes, duties, imposts, and excises."

The historical definition of "general welfare" focused more on protecting the citizens' rights, but the general welfare today can also include welfare and entitlement programs designed to ensure that all citizens have the wherewithal to enjoy their rights.

Habeas Corpus

Habeas corpus ("that you have the body") originated as a legal principle in England's Magna Carta. Before that time, the king had the untrammeled power to have people detained arbitrarily. Habeas corpus gave every individual the right to appear before a judge to contest imprisonment.

Habeas corpus appears in the US Constitution in Article 1, Section 9, Clause 2: "The Privilege of the Writ of Habeas Corpus shall not be suspended, unless when in cases of Rebellion or Invasion the public Safety may require it." Habeas corpus is therefore an explicitly foundational element of American due process—even after conviction.

Justice

Justice can be defined as the equal and fair treatment of all people under the law. The Preamble to the Constitution tells us that establishing justice was one of the founders' reasons for their successful effort to "ordain and establish this Constitution for the United States of America."

A court may determine that a law is unjust. Then the law is effectively nullified, and the court is not obliged to enforce it. Such rulings have occurred frequently during and since the civil rights movement. On the legislative side, Congress has often amended laws to help ensure more equal and just treatment for all.

Liberty

Liberty is one of the inalienable rights cited in the Declaration of Independence. It refers to the right of the individual to act according to his or her will. The Bill of Rights lists many "Blessings of Liberty" as freedoms. Freedoms often recognized by the courts include freedom of choice, freedom of action, and freedom from arbitrary and unreasonable physical restraint.

The definition of liberty remains broad today. A 1954 Supreme Court opinion (*Bolling v. Sharpe*) stated that "'liberty' . . . is not confined to mere freedom from bodily restraint. Liberty under law extends to the full range of conduct which the individual is free to pursue, and it cannot be restricted except for a proper governmental objective."

Privacy

The word "privacy" does not appear in our founding documents. The Bill of Rights, however, cites many freedoms which we today think of as private rights. The word "privacy" finally appeared in a legal context in an 1890 law review article entitled "The Right to Privacy," which contended that the individual had a "right to be left alone."

Today, US law can be said to address six broad flavors of privacy: physical, decisional, proprietary, associational, intellectual, and informational. We have focused in this book on informational privacy.

Everyone has his or her own definition of privacy. I define privacy as my right to enjoy my physical and spiritual spaces. Such enjoyment is possible only in a democratic society where everyone respects and supports privacy. Such respect guarantees that one's home is one's sanctuary. It allows one to be alone with one's thoughts, both written and unwritten. It recognizes each person's right to keep those thoughts in reserve or share them with others. Such respect should extend to personal information in cyberspace.

Republic: See Democracy.

Right to Petition

The right to petition came from the Magna Carta, England's first Constitution. It gave every individual the right to appear before officials to report any offense and ask for things to be set right. Our forefathers included it in the First Amendment as the right "to petition the Government for a redress of grievances."

This right has broadened in modern times to mean that citizens can ask the government for anything, including redress. People have the right to petition their elected officials in Congress with their thoughts and demands about government (*Eastern RR Presidents Conf. v. Noerr Motor Freight*, 1961). People also have the right to petition the government to exercise its powers when other entities affect the petitioners' interests. See also Freedom of Assembly.

We the People

This phrase occurs in the opening words of the US Constitution: "WE THE PEOPLE of the United States . . . do ordain and establish this Constitution for the United States of America." The term "We the People" refers to the citizens of the United States who collectively establish and authorize the federal government to act on their behalf as specified in—and restricted by—the Constitution.

The original intent of this phrase remains today.

Index

Printed in the USA
CPSIA information can be obtained
at www.ICGtesting.com
JSHW010845251023
50683JS00024B/111/J